TR

In the same series

The Right Way To Conduct Meetings
Your Voice: How To Enrich It, And Develop It For Speaking, Acting And Everyday Conversation

Uniform with this book

THE HON. TREASURER

Roderick Boucher

Typeset in 10/11½pt Times by County Typesetters, Margate, Kent.

Printed and bound in Great Britain by Cox & Wyman Ltd., Reading, Berkshire.

The *Right Way* series and the *Paperfronts* series are both published by Elliot Right Way Books, Brighton Road, Lower Kingswood, Tadworth, Surrey, KT20 6TD, U.K.

CONTENTS

CHAPTER		PAGE
1	Getting Started	7
2	Controls	16
3	The Cash Book	33
4	Changing Your Bank Account	55
5	Planning	59
6	Meetings and Reporting	72
7	Financial Techniques	80
8	Tips On Finance For Small Scale Events	94
9	Receipts and Payments Accounts	99
10	Beyond Receipts and Payments Accounts	104
11	The Audit	121
Appendix 1	Starting From Scratch	123
Appendix 2	Explanatory Notes on Accounting Jargon	126
Appendix 3	Double Entry Book Keeping	137
Index		156

1
GETTING STARTED

You have accepted the role of Hon. Treasurer. Where do you start?

Appointment

First. Find out how and when you are to be appointed. Very often this will not be until the Annual General Meeting. Do not sign anything until you are sure that you really are the Treasurer.

Keep a copy of the appointment minute for future reference. Acting prematurely almost certainly renders you personally liable for what you do and could cause annoyance, especially if the old Treasurer has a change of heart at the last minute and decides to stay on.

Collect The Books and Records

First look at the cash book and bank account. What is the cash position? Is there enough cash in hand for you to take some time understanding the general picture? If not, see the previous Treasurer and bank manager as a matter of urgency.

Bank Mandates and Signatories

The bank mandate is the form which the organisation fills in to instruct the bank as to how its business is to be done – how many people are needed to sign cheques, who they are.

Find out the terms of the bank mandates in place. Who are the other signatories? Why? Are they all still doing the jobs they were when they became signatories? Normally you would expect several of the other officers or committee members to be authorised to sign cheques and for two signatures to be required in all cases.

Lay hands on all the cheque books and make sure that there are no informal arrangements whereby the Chairman, steward, barman, cleaner, or anyone else, holds a stack of signed blank cheques, 'Just in case they need to pay something urgently.'

Rule of thumb for the right number of signatories is more than 4 and less than 7. Too few and they will all be away on holiday when you need them. Too many and the task may not be seen as the responsible job of supervision and safeguarding that it is.

Where do they live? Note full names, addresses and phone numbers in the 'permanent file' that already has your appointment authority in it. There will be a night when you need an urgent signature. A short walk is much better than a 20 mile drive. Both are better than discovering that the one person available is ex-directory and you can't remember exactly where he lives. In my last role I was blessed with one signatory, a few minutes drive away, who was never in before 9 p.m. but was always available after then until midnight.

Ask the others to give you a rough outline of their normal availability. This can save multiple phone calls trying to set up appointments for cheque signing. There is a temptation for treasurers to use normal meetings to get this job done. This can be effective but prevents two people from listening to what members have to say at the one time they get an opportunity to say it. I have always found the informal communication that goes with getting the cheques counter-signed on a one to one basis, usually at home, to be a worthwhile investment of time.

List all the different accounts. Prepare new mandates for each one. Remember to reflect other changes in the committee and officers. Prepare a motion for the next meeting to approve those signatories. Ideally this would be covered and minuted immediately following your appointment.

What Is It?

Are you looking after a private club, a registered charity, the branch of a charity, a sports club, a church?

What special rules govern the organisation? Who is it accountable to? Is there a manual? What returns have to be made to whom and when? Is it registered for VAT? Does it pay tax?

Job Description: Roles and Responsibilities

Ask for a job description. The odds are against there being one, but it will concentrate the committee's mind on what they really want you to do. Although the job of Treasurer sounds fairly easy to define, there may be both unexpected ingredients and boundary disputes. I was initially taken aback to find that my name appeared on all the raffles organised under our team churches' lottery licence, even more so when I looked at the penalties involved in getting it wrong. Boundary disputes work both ways. There may be duties you believe are appropriate to the Treasurer alone. Equally there may be some duties which you would like to avoid.

Who is responsible for?

- estimating property insurance values
- insurance claims administration
- collecting members' subs
- covenant recording
- contract review
- purchasing policy
- rent collection and tenancy agreements
- setting rates for the use of the hall

Use the discussion of who does what to open up the chance to change. Encourage people to say what they think and to give you new ideas. Look for opportunities to spread the load, to develop, train, delegate and, most important, to start the search for your successor. Consider the possibility of a deputy.

Handover

Meet with your predecessor. You may decide in due course that he cut corners, specialised in unintelligible journal entries, spilt coffee all over the accounts, and filed all the vouchers back to front. You are going to improve efficiency and do things differently. Of course you are, but hold all critical comments for about 12 months, preferably much longer.

He may be prepared to give you holiday or emergency cover.

He is the one person who can give you a feel for the pressure spots and the people involved – from a Treasurer's point of view.

What does the job entail?

What parts are enjoyable?

What were the nasty moments?

Who can be trusted?

Who needs watching?

Who can be left to get on with a project with a rough outline approval?

Who should be supervised in detail?

What was the daily, weekly, monthly routine?

It is useful to have at least two handover sessions, one to get the general impression of the job, a second to go through detailed questions that arise from going through the accounts.

Accounting Records and Working Papers

Get hold of the records of the previous years. They should include the cash book, bank statements and the supporting vouchers – paid bills, correspondence, minutes, scraps of paper. The next step is part audit, part detective story.

Start reading. Stay awake. The last two years' invoices and general paperwork will tell you as much as, or more than, the handover.

BANK STATEMENTS

How many entries per week? How often is the money paid into the bank? Are there regular transfers to and from the deposit account? What kind of balance is usually in hand?

Are there any bank charges? How often does the account get overdrawn? How many standing orders or direct debits are there and how often? Is interest paid on the current account? What rate is the deposit account earning?

Look also for returned cheques. Normal errors and accidents usually account for a couple in any year but more than that could point to some nasty situations and hassle. Make some rough notes of what you see and file them with the bank mandates.

EXPENSE VOUCHERS

What is the process for telling the Treasurer that the bills are O.K. to pay? Which bills were red? Why? Who are the frequent suppliers? How many disputes were there over late payment, shoddy work, incorrect deliveries and who sorted them out? Which names keep coming up? How adequate are the scraps of paper presented to the Treasurer to request reimbursement? Which people tend to present supermarket till rolls for their normal shopping with a few items circled in red to indicate that they were for the fête or jumble sale? Conversely, who always provides a clear lucid explanation of their purchases with full back-up?

Try to build a picture in your mind of the events that made these payments happen.

RECEIPTS VOUCHERS

What receipts are there? Who counts and banks the money? Is it always the same person? Is a record kept of all cheques received? Is every receipt recorded and acknowledged?

Are the levels of subscription clear? Are they annual, monthly, weekly or completely irregular? What patterns can you see? When are the busy periods?

Group the receipts into logical areas and look for procedures or lack of them. Note down the main headings, for example:

Subscriptions
Hall lettings
Fund raising events
Donations
Cash for coffee and biscuits
Rent
Appeals

CASH BOOK

Look at the overall layout. You should be able to read the pages now with a broad understanding of what you see. If you have ploughed through a couple of years' vouchers, the cash book entries will probably be old friends.

How easy is it to check cash book entries with the bank statements? Is the cash book analysed into main expenditure and income headings? Are all the entries in 'miscellaneous'?

Can you understand the business in the most general sense just by looking at the cash book? If you can, be grateful for a good predecessor. If 'No' think about how you can change for the better.

LEDGERS

Are there any? Try to work out what their specific purpose is. How and when are the entries made? Who controls them?

The Published Accounts

Obtain copies of as many previous years as you can. At least seven ought to be available for legal reasons.

Reviewing the accounts has two objectives:

- identifying trends and changes
- checking the financial position which you have taken on.

TRENDS AND CHANGES

As a start, take the simplest of views. Jot down on a piece of paper – a single sheet – total income, total expense, total assets, net assets and cash for each year. Round the figures to thousands or hundreds of pounds so that you can strip out spurious detail. How have the figures changed? Is there a steady growth in both income and expenses? Which were the funny years which don't fit the trend? Are there any trends at all? What looks peculiar?

Next look at the headings sub-dividing income and expense. Are they the same every year? Is the answer to a peculiarity in the first exercise a special one-off activity? Again it is useful to schedule out in columns the analysis of income and expense and to look at the comparative figures, suitably rounded, to get a feel for the general direction, the start of new activities and the end of old ones.

The story may be quite simple.

'Things muddled along quietly until the savings, which used to earn interest, were spent on the car park. Every year since has been a struggle.'

'Most years contain a big project and the fund raising is driven up to match the needs.'

'Membership subs have risen to match expenses.'

They may be simple, more often there are some more stories behind the figures: an energetic Chairman, a team of people who worked together well but have all just reached retirement age.

Take what the figures appear to show and ask for clarification of the background. Testing your understanding and deciding what it means for your role is vital. More of this later but, if the previous seven years show absolutely no evidence of the membership being able to produce the funds for a major improvement project, you will need some convincing when the first batch of bright and expensive ideas comes in.

CHECKING THE FINANCIAL POSITION

The balance sheet, sometimes known as the statement of affairs, is the financial position you are taking over responsibility for. It is essential to satisfy yourself of its validity early on in the job.

Fixed Assets

What are they? Where are they? How much are they really worth? Where is the evidence of ownership? When will they need replacement and how much will they cost?

If land, freehold or leasehold property is involved, why not take a look at the deeds and see where the boundaries are? They should be in safe-keeping and it does no harm to inspect things to make sure that the bank or solicitor has not lost them.

For office equipment there should be a register with serial numbers and details of original cost. Look at it. Physical inspection confirms both that it really exists and what kind of condition it is in. You may also find things which are owned but not recorded in the accounts. Sometimes donated items are worth more than purchased ones.

Make a schedule, if there is not one already, and file it for review of the insurance cover later.

Investments

What are they? Who holds the share certificates? Again they should be in a place of safe-keeping. Get written confirmation from bank or solicitors. Better still, go and see them. Are there any restrictions on selling them? Are there rules laid down for how this should be done? If not, set them up now rather than when the need is urgent.

Are they good long term investments? Who is the best person to decide that? Do they conform to legal requirements as to the kind of investments which are allowed to be held?

How much are they really worth now? Check with a recent copy of 'The Financial Times' or 'The Daily Telegraph'.

Can you see any income from the investments in the accounts? If not where is it? In one case there was a deposit of £400 shown in the accounts with no income. Follow-up produced a separately administered fund and a property which no-one in the 'committee' knew anything about. No income from an investment can also, of course, mean that the investment is not there.

Debtors

Who are they? What for? How old are the debts? When will they be paid?

Pre-payments

What for? Check the calculations and the back-up. Was it necessary to pay in advance? Is there a case for spreading payment?

Cash

How much? What rate of interest is it earning? Is it in the right place? There are still thousands of pounds of charitable and club money in old-fashioned current accounts and deposit accounts earning no or tiny rates of interest.

For charities there are a number of 'Common Investment Funds'. Details are available from 'The Official Custodian for Charities' c/o the Charity Commission. These provide a range of options for short or long term investment, including access to good rates on simple deposits. They offer professional management which would be unaffordable for small organisations with limited funds. The 1992 Charities Act allows wider powers of investment than before. Finding the best return is difficult, but it may be possible to double the rate as the first step and worry about the half percents later.

If you are not looking after a charity it is still worth a discussion with bank or building society to check that the current deal is the best available.

Creditors

Who are they? When should they be paid? Talk to the previous Treasurer rather than the man you owe the money to. Are there contractual difficulties? Has the work been done to everyone's satisfaction? The creditor balance could be monies held on retention because the new car park doubles as a duck pond whenever it rains. It could be an amount of money which is disputed. Often creditors contain the juiciest bits of history in the whole accounts. It is worth mastering the full story early on. It will also give insight on the way things have been done in the past.

Funds

Initially ask for evidence of objectives, conditions, trustees and rules. If there are special funds you need to understand why they exist, how they are managed and what their purpose is. Rely on common sense and take time to understand the facts. See, touch, ask, test and make sure for yourself.

Minutes

Obtain and read the minutes of committee meetings for as far back as you can get hold of and bear to go. They should tell you about debates, arguments, commitments, decisions, projects under way, contractual problems, and throw extra light on what you have already learned from review of the accounts.

Auditor and Advisors

Meet with the auditor and ask if there are any concerns or recommendations which he feels you should be aware of, big or small. Find out the extent to which he is prepared to advise you through the year rather than after the year-end. He may be happy to be available on the end of the phone to help you solve a problem if it gives him an easier job in the long run. If there is a solicitor, architect, or any other special advisor, make contact to let them know of your appointment and give them the opportunity to tell you of any problems they think you should know about.

Consider the overall quality and range of expert advice

available. Discuss with the rest of the committee how to go about filling any gaps that you can see.

Status

You have now read the detailed story. As a test, write down what you think happens for the main events and processes, including who does what to whom. Use it in your next handover review. If it is confirmed, you have an outline manual. Often your impressions will be corrected. Update your notes if they are, but also be alert; some of your concerns will be spot on and need dealing with. One of the great values in having a new person on the job is the fresh perceptions and insights, unblunted by getting used to things the way they always have been.

By now you should have a good idea of the job, the organisation, procedures or lack of them, and the financial status. Write down on an action sheet all your questions, concerns and ideas for change. Leave space to track the answers. Keep it and refer back to it regularly to check on progress and update your first impressions.

2
CONTROLS

There should be little need to preach about the reasons to have good controls. There is:

FRAUD

No matter how many previously innocent people are convicted of defrauding charities, the mentality of voluntary organisations is often, 'It could not happen here.' Even churches, which know all about fallibility and frailty, work on the principle that human nature applies to the whole human race, but not the members of their own congregation.

TURNOVER OF PEOPLE

Some volunteers serve one cause faithfully for many years. However, they are always free agents and it is not that uncommon for people to get annoyed and leave. People move for jobs, a better house, school catchment area. Circumstances change: redundancy, sickness, children growing up, business failure. Any or all of these can happen to the least likely people. The challenge is to have an operation that gets the best out of new faces quickly and does not fall apart when old ones leave.

MISTAKES

A great thing about volunteer work is being allowed to have a crack at something you know nothing about. Anyone willing will find themselves involved in new and exciting tasks. The down side of this freedom is the risk of failure and mistake.

Controls are about having an approach to money and possessions which takes into account the real risks – of temptation, change and of mistake – that are around in any human process. Control awareness leads to ways of organising so that errors are picked up promptly and opportunities for fraud are severely limited. It means identifying weaknesses and building a web of support to counter them. Good controls protect individuals from the possibility of wrongdoing. Just as important, they also protect the individual from accusation of wrongdoing. Here ends the sermon.

Income

By far the biggest problem is the point where the money comes in. For each type of income find out:

* how the money arrives
* who receives it
* who records what is received
* how we would know if we did not get the money.

VOLUNTARY COLLECTIONS

At its simplest level this could be a 'whip round' for a present for a retiring president. Receipts are inappropriate: the donors may go to great lengths to avoid anyone knowing how much they have given. Public appeals, church collections, going round with a collection bucket at a charity football match, school fêtes, all have the same problem. The figures cannot be verified by outside reference.

The solution here is to build the controls at the point the organisation receives the cash. That does not mean stuffing the Treasurer away in a cubby hole until he comes out with a full biscuit tin and a scruffy note of a total. There is little point in guarding the collection like Fort Knox in public and then handing it over to one person to count in private. That person has no defence if someone claims that the full amount collected did not get as far as the bank or the beneficiary.

There must be more than one person involved whenever unrecorded cash is being handled. This is required by law for street collections. All boxes and tins have to be opened by at least two people. It is a good idea even when the law does not require it. Once counted, the result should be recorded and minuted. Your insurance policy may well only cover cash after it has been counted. When it is counted and recorded it becomes less of an issue because you have some evidence to say how much there was and you can spot if it goes missing. Refuse to do the job alone and make sure no-one else does either.

Examples of good control are:

* A church where different people assist with communion each week. They also act as the counting team.
* At a fête a counting team of three allows for one person to be caught short or to fetch the essential cup of tea. Four is even better – two to guard the hoard and two to go round collecting it from stallholders.

FUND-RAISING

Fund-raising is voluntary collections with a twist. If someone agrees to hold a coffee morning at home for club funds, along with a bring and buy sale, how can you possibly control it?

Ask that any such projects be reviewed with you at the planning stage. That allows you to make a decision as to the amount of money likely to be involved and the risk that goes with it. For a coffee morning you may simply ask that the amount be certified by a second independent person. Give a receipt. Publish the result and get it in the minutes. Get the control message over positively. It is to protect people as much as to check up on them. Here is a story from a few years ago:

A family of four ran a bogus appeal, collecting money from the public using the name of a charitable cause, complete with specially opened bank account. They raised about £10,000 but paid over less than £500.

The organisation has the absolute right to turn down offers of fund-raising efforts that they are not happy about. A more general point is that you ought to find out about the new faces before you hand them the cash tin. Once I was invited to become Treasurer on the strength of a chat over coffee. 'You don't know me from Adam' I said, 'how do you know you can trust me?' 'We've met your in-laws', they replied.

Why not ask for references? Another recent story:

A bookkeeper stole £17,000 from his charity. He was taken on without references but had previous convictions for, amongst other things, fraud.

HALL LETTINGS

Split the job up. Have one person handle the bookings and another handle the money. Have the Bookings Secretary keep a diary that shows who has used the hall. Keep a duplicate receipts book and enter full details for every user.

As Treasurer, make a periodic inspection of the diary to confirm that the money you are receiving looks about right.

If the income is regular, use printed and numbered bookings forms. Print the normal lettings prices and put any special deals in writing. For users who have the same slot every week think about asking for payment by cheque or standing order.

SUBSCRIPTIONS

This area provides a world in miniature. It contains most of the problems of controlling income and can be solved in a variety of valid ways. It is something everyone can relate to and think of their own examples for. My best case of how not to do it was the charity branch with around 20 members on the register and an annual subscription of £5. Subscription income for the year was £65. The Chairman collected the subs but half way through the year the records, showing how much each member gave, stopped being filled in.

Who should do what?

You can introduce control by delegating work. If you, the Treasurer, collect the subs each week in cash, enter up the cash book, and pay the money into the bank, there is no independent check. That makes you part of the problem. The auditor should be having nightmares, even if you are an upright and reputable citizen. Getting someone else to collect and count gives an independent check. You can look at the amounts coming in and compare them with what you expect and believe reasonable.

Evidence

Knowing what is reasonable does not tell you 100% that you are getting all the subscriptions that are collected or that the amount collected is all that should have been. To know that, you need a record that tells you the amount due. This can be a membership book, a membership list with membership numbers, a register, a computer spreadsheet, or just counting up the number of people there on the night. Preferably this record should be kept by someone other than the person collecting the cash, or at least checked on the spot and signed by a second person. Otherwise the control is useless because the record can be 'adapted' to the amount of money handed over.

Keeping evidence like this also introduces a control on the Treasurer – the auditor has something to check the bankings with and the membership secretary has the information to know whether the amount that is shown for 'Subs' in the annual accounts is about right.

Cash, cheques and standing orders

Cash is slippery stuff. It is heavy, hard to control, easy to lose and a hassle to count, especially those 5p coins that refuse to stack in piles of 20. Cheques carry names and can be made relatively safe. The best policy is to ask anyone paying by cheque to:

a) cross them
b) write 'Account payee only, not negotiable' between the lines of the crossing.

Remember to tell them in plain English whom the cheque should be made out to, otherwise the bank will refuse to accept it. The objective, unlike the 'Free Prize Draw' mailshots, is to make it easy for people to see what they have to do.

A separate paragraph in the letter notifying of membership fees, stating **Cheques should be made payable to '365th Najafabad Scouts'** is much better than hiding it or not actually telling anyone the name of the account.

The bank will then only pay the cheque into the account named on the cheque. They will not pay it into an account with a different name, or accept an endorsement on the back to pay it to cash. Standing orders are better still. The money goes directly into the account. Almost all of it will arrive on time and problems will be easy to spot. It may make sense to have a separate 'subscriptions' account so that your normal operating account is not strewn with odd names that make reconciliation a pain. Using cheques and standing orders rather than cash brings the bank's records into play as a control tool. So, if you can move your membership onto paying their subscriptions annually, in advance, by standing order, you will be almost there. It also improves cash flow. The drawback is the work involved in changing the standing orders for increases in subscriptions or moving bank accounts.

Agree the rules

The subscription level, circumstances where reduced fees are payable, new joining fee, part year subscription, and the procedure for dealing with non-payers should all be agreed by the committee and, where appropriate, published. You need confidentiality but you also need evidence for audit. That could be a minute saying that a certain number of subscription waivers had been approved, with the names kept confidential. What you do not want is a situation where the Chairman decides unilaterally not to collect subscriptions from people he deems to be needy without being able to remember who or how much.

Putting the process together

Use the control tools and guidelines to come up with a system that works efficiently and with minimum effort. Having designed it, the next job is to write up the process so that someone new could pick up any of the jobs without difficulty. The first one you draft may be rejected, perhaps you have gone overboard on control to the point where the process is clumsy and hard work. Revise it until you have something which is practical and understood. If there are still some risks uncovered, spell them out. Review it and change it if bugs are discovered. (See sample below.)

Membership Subscriptions Process (Annual)

People involved: Membership Secretary, Membership Treasurer, Treasurer, Chairman

TASK	RESPONSIBLE	TARGET DATE
1. Agree next year's subscription rate and publish.	Treasurer/ committee	31/10
2. Prepare membership master list. Provide details of deletions and new members. List to contain: full name, current address membership number, subscription due (copies to Membership Treasurer & Treasurer)	Mem Sec	12/11
3. Draft subscription letter.	Mem Treasurer	12/11
4. Approve subs letter.	Chairman & Treasurer	19/11
5. Send out subscription letters and membership cards.	Mem Sec	30/11
6. Receive subscriptions. Record and pay into bank. Note of bankings to Treasurer. Prepare monthly report of amounts received & still due.	Mem Treasurer	31/1 28/2 31/3
7. Pass list of non-payers to Membership Secretary and Treasurer for follow up.	Mem Treasurer	30/4

TASK	RESPONSIBLE	TARGET DATE
8. Investigation of non-payment & recommendation to committee.	Mem Sec & Treasurer	31/5
9. Report on membership subs status.	Treasurer	as required
Membership Subscriptions Process (Ongoing)		
1. Enrol new members and report to committee. Provide full names and details to Membership Treasurer and Treasurer.	Mem Sec	Monthly
2. Send subscription letter to new members.	Mem Sec	On acceptance.
3. Receive subs. Pay into bank and report to Treasurer.	Mem Treas	Monthly

Note that the Treasurer does comparatively little in this system. He checks, makes sure things happen on time, and deals with problems. The Membership Treasurer has a specific job which is busy for a limited period only. It is also a good training role for a future Treasurer.

Control strengths are:

Duties are divided between three different people: in particular the Membership Secretary provides the master records but does not get anywhere near the cash; the Membership Treasurer handles cheques and cash but is controlled by the master list and the reports; the Treasurer knows how much to expect. Disputes over whether individual members have paid or not paid are out in the open because they are reported to the Treasurer and Membership Secretary for action.

This is just an example of what might be appropriate for a fairly large club. It can also be effective for quite small numbers. My son's Scout group issues subscription letters each term and operates most of the controls above for around 70 boys. They chase late payers, like me, and get the money in efficiently.

Weekly subs might be entered in a register against members' names, totalled at the bottom and the cash handed to the Treasurer to bank or put in the safe with a note as to how much it was. You would still want to use the 'more than one' principle for counting the cash and have a counter signature in the register. For 'subscriptions' read rent, or any other amount which is receivable on a regular basis and has to be collected.

COVENANTS

The additional dimension to covenant payments is the requirement to prove that payment has been made. One year the Inland Revenue inspected several dioceses of the Church of England. They checked all the records for each and every covenant in some parishes and demanded repayments of tax from the whole diocese on the basis of the percentage of claims found to be not in order, plus, of course, interest and penalties.

The burden is on the charity to prove that the covenanted money has been given. Cheques, bankers' orders, envelope schemes are acceptable. Loose cash in the plate is not.

There are now a range of options for tax effective charitable giving, some of them easier to control than covenants – Payroll giving and Gift Aid for example. If the risk is having to pay back the tax reclaimed on covenanted giving, it is too serious for any charity, however small, to ignore. If you look after a branch of a large charity then the head office should produce guidance and, probably, the necessary paperwork.

Points to consider for good controls are:

1. Appointing a separate 'Stewardship Treasurer' gives an independent check. It is a job with its own peak workloads, requiring conscientiousness and, above all, discretion.
2. The records of receipts must prove that the money was given.
3. The Stewardship Treasurer should review progress and make sure the donor does not fail to pay the covenanted amount for lack of a gentle reminder.
4. Review the Stewardship Treasurer's records and system periodically to make sure they are adequate. If you cannot prove that the amounts covenanted have been physically paid, legally you should not reclaim the tax.

If all that seems hard, think about getting your donors to use one of the 'Charities Aid Foundation' schemes. Their address is in Appendix 1. Good control can mean recognising that the effort outweighs the benefit and going for the easy way out.

INSURANCE CLAIMS

Instances of damage or accident giving rise to a claim should be minuted at meetings and responsibility given for the repairs and the insurance claim to named individuals. Ask for a brief status report on progress at each meeting. At all costs, avoid the situation where everyone thinks someone else is handling it.

Get a claim file set up which holds and records:

Date and nature of the accident or damage
Date of notification to insurance company (or agent)
Claim form
Repairs/replacement cost estimates
Confirmation from insurance company of acceptance of estimate and authority to go ahead with repairs.

There can be long delays between the original damage and the final repair, replacement and repayment. A well put together file, with all the correspondence and notes of phone calls, protects the organisation when the individuals change, for whatever reason. If the claim is large and complex, decide up front who has responsibility and power to make decisions, perhaps a sub-committee, perhaps the whole committee.

GRANTS

With loose cash, especially the new small coins, it requires a lot of hard work to lose large sums of money. With a grant, one piece of paper – the cheque – could be worth thousands.

I did pick up one case as an auditor where a grant cheque was accidentally paid into the Treasurer's personal deposit account. Fortunately my audit picked up the fact that the grant had been claimed and the Chairman knew that it had been paid, so the error was found and corrected quickly. Fortunately also, it was for a relatively small sum.

Experience on other grant situations suggests these problems:

- poor communication in committee about the fact that a grant is being applied for. Sometimes only one person knows anything about it.
- little advance planning to ensure that work being done meets requirements for grant eligibility. The biggest culprit is having started the work before approval is given. That is usually the kiss of death to the application.
- time limits not being observed.

There is one other obvious sin of omission: not thinking about grants in the first place. It is well worth appointing one committee member to do some research on local and national trusts and grant making bodies so that the opportunity is highlighted rather than ignored. If you are tackling a £20,000 plus project, one £10,000 grant saves upwards of 70 jumble sales.

The control approach is to get organised so that accidents and errors either are prevented, or picked up routinely and quickly and corrected. Accidents and errors are wider than someone absconding with the cash and include things which do not go in the accounts. No accounting system reports on the fact that £5,000 was lost to the organisation because some clown set the builders off too early (no-one had told him that a grant was being applied for), or because a local council application deadline had been missed.

RESUMÉ – INCOME CONTROLS

Cash

* **Always to be counted by more than one person**
* **Receipts given as standard**
* **Document the result immediately**
* **Avoid it – cheques are safer**
  Cheques marked 'ACCOUNT PAYEE ONLY' are better
  Standing Orders are even better still.

People

* **Delegate**
  (Makes you part of the solution not the problem)
* **Work through controls not trust**

Expense Controls

PROTECTING THE ORGANISATION FROM YOU

The first person the organisation should worry about is you, the Treasurer, or anyone else in a role that involves holding the organisation's cheques and the ability to write them out and sign them. That also covers the ability to instruct the bank to transfer cash from the bank account. It is less easy for money to go walkabout without trace once it has got into the bank account. This is probably the most publicised fraud – the one that involves the Treasurer ripping off the organisation. A recent story:

> *Charity Treasurer jailed for false accounting. He stole more than £50,000 to pay his mortgage. His wife was also an officer and was found guilty of the same offence.*

TWO SIGNATURES

The first line of defence is to insist on all cheques being

signed by two people. The second signature makes it hard for the Treasurer to pay his own personal bills out of organisation funds. The particular temptation seems to be with bills for gas and electricity.

It also gives you, the Treasurer, protection from that accusation. Treasurer's family do not make appropriate cheque signatories. Kind second signatories, who sign blank cheques to make the Treasurer's life easier, are to be avoided. Another recent case:

> *Founder of charity went missing after withdrawing over £100,000 from the bank account. Her co-trustee had signed blank cheques in all good faith.*

USING BUDGETS

A benefit, if you operate a budget system, is that you have laid down who you expect to spend money, and how much. Those with budgets should know what they can or cannot do without needing to come back to you for approval. A good plan lays out clearly what is on the shopping list and roughly when the money will be spent. If you want to keep a percentage of the budget back, take it through committee and tell budget holders where they stand.

> 'The agreed budget for Junior Church this year is £150: £75 for course books and materials and £75 for new bibles. Please check with me before ordering the bibles as we may need to postpone this item until next year.'

That gives the individual the chance to argue the point and you the ability to take the decision at the right time. Much better than complaining afterwards.

PETTY CASH

A petty cash system recognises that someone needs to be able to spend small amounts regularly. There is usually one person who is the obvious candidate: Secretary, Administrator, or Caretaker.

Avoid having a petty cash account if you can. It means more analysis and work to look after it. If the people who need to spend out are happy to put in their expenses and wait a few days for the cheque, there is no need to run a petty cash book.

If not, then operate a petty cash system.

The Petty Cash Float

Choose an amount which ought to cover cash expenditure for

a month; a round sum like £20 or £50 will do. This is given to your 'spender' in cash. (One of the few cases where it is appropriate to make a cheque out to 'Cash'.) Give them the cash and get a receipt. Place it on file. 'Received £50 as petty cash float on 2nd November (year)'.

The float, which should be kept in a locked box, must be kept distinct by the spender at all times. As they spend the cash they must write down each item in a petty cash book and keep the vouchers. This book does not need many columns but it should explain what everything was bought for and be numbered – PC/(yr)/1, PC/(yr)/2, PC/(yr)/3. It is basically a second cash book.

When the cash is running low they ask for a cheque to take the float back up to the target level. The spend in the petty cash book is totalled and that is the amount paid over. Take the opportunity to inspect the petty cash book and analyse the expense according to your own classification of different expense types. Finally, prepare a single sheet summary for your records. You sign the petty cash book to indicate that you have been through it and the petty cash 'spender' countersigns your summary voucher to record that they spent that amount and have received the re-imbursement cheque. The vouchers can either be filed by you or the petty cash 'spender', but they must be kept as they are a basic record and evidence, and will be required by the auditor.

The test is that you or the auditor, or someone else if you delegate the job, should be able to go to the petty cash holder at any time and ask to count the petty cash. The actual cash in hand plus the value of vouchers for money spent must always add up to the petty cash advance.

ONE OFF SMALL EXPENSES

Wherever possible, invoices should be obtained which actually say what has been bought. If the organisation is registered for VAT, not getting invoices will mean not being able to reclaim input VAT but, even if VAT is not involved, the evidence a VAT inspector would want to see is a good yardstick. With a little explanation most people will understand that you need invoices and receipts for your records. If the goods are the sort that most families buy every week – like the wherewithal for a barn dance supper – ask

a) for an organiser to countersign the claim to confirm that the goods were for that purpose.
b) for the goods to be on a separate invoice from the ordinary shopping.

c) for a plain English note explaining what the expenditure was for.

With all these small value expenses the object of the controls described is to make sure that the money was actually incurred on behalf of the organisation and to provide evidence that lets the auditor confirm it. These controls do not guarantee the money was spent wisely, nor that the things bought were the best deal going. Handling lots of small items it would be unreasonable to insist on this. You probably have not reimbursed the cost of getting to the shops, you cannot pay for the trouble, so discourage the 'experts' who complain that the bread rolls would have been cheaper elsewhere.

LARGE VALUE ITEMS

Where the question of value for money and spending wisely does have to be covered is with the big spends. Large value can be both a single big project, or a contract to buy something regularly over a long period. Getting the best price on heating oil can save hundreds of pounds over the years.

Decisions Not Accidents

> 'The old duplicator has had it. Terrible results and messy. Why don't we buy our own photocopier? It would be much more convenient and we could produce our own newsletters. We could charge it out to other people and make a profit. I've had a quote of 3p per copy, that would save us 40% of what we pay today.'

Fine; get information on the costs of the different options. Check on the truth of the statements.

Put the figures down on paper and talk it through. Ask if there are any members with particular expertise who can give guidance. Where does this fit on the priority list? What impact does it have on the cash position and all the other things people want to do or buy?

Another phrase for this proper review of facts is a 'business case'. See under Financial Techniques (page 89).

Contracts

Contracts are a potential nightmare. Here are some actual blunders.

Copier lease signed with finance house before terms were confirmed in writing and without a contract for service and maintenance. The supplier also claimed to be operating under a special approved charitable purchasing scheme. They were not.

Building contract signed by someone who was not legally able to sign on behalf of the organisation, for a sum 20% higher than the funding available.

Professional advisers commissioned to do work (and charge their fees) without the knowledge or approval of the committee.

Maintenance contract cancelled and order placed with competitor for cheaper price and equivalent service. An officer kindly signs a contract renewal with the first supplier when asked to by the rep.

Let us rehearse the wisdom of the ages.

1. Invite tenders or quotes from more than one supplier.
2. Ask for, and take up before making your decision, references of work done satisfactorily elsewhere.
3. Check out the local reputation of the supplier, or preferably use it to select the people you ask to tender in the first place.
4. Read the contract, **including the small print**.
5. Understand the rights specified in the contract to increase prices over the contract period.
6. If you do not understand the contract get someone who does to read it and explain it, and that does not mean the salesman.
7. Put any questions or specifications in writing and get assurances in writing too.
8. Get quotations rather than estimates.
9. Work out what going ahead means to cash flow and budgets.
10. Ask yourself if the priorities are right. Does spending money on this project prevent other, more needed, things from going ahead?

All familiar and old hat to everyone. So why is it that so many cases happen where a totally different agenda is followed? Namely:

'The salesman seems a nice guy. Let's order it quick. We don't want to miss the special offer.'
'I'm sure they are a reliable firm.'
'It's a great machine. What does it do exactly?'

'What contract? You mean that piece of paper I signed?'
'Who was responsible for getting us into this mess?'
'I thought the Treasurer had checked it.'

There should be an absolute prohibition on anyone signing a contract or making a commitment without proper approval. Very nice people – they are the ones who will do anything and sign anything to oblige the salesman and avoid an unpleasant incident – need to be even more afraid of what will happen to them if they sign than if they don't.

I do not believe all salesmen are sharks or cowboys. The best will try to identify a solution and product that is mutually beneficial to them and their customer, but,

'It's surprising how often the customers' interest and my quota objectives happen to co-incide.'

There is no law against being prepared. Before anyone gets the salesman in, get the organisation's needs and wants straight in everyone's mind. Write down the criteria you want to use to score what you are being offered.

Become an intelligent buyer: take in the sales pitch; thank the salesman for his time; ask him to excuse you for a few minutes while you talk it through; invite him back in to deal with more questions and then sleep on it. When you have slept on it go through steps 1 to 9 above.

So what usually happens? Someone on the committee is convinced that this is the right product. He makes all the claims for it and takes over the sales pitch. He gets the discussion going with the salesman present and defers to him as a consultant. He squashes opposition and sees no reason for not placing the order immediately. If it turns out to be a lemon it was a committee decision and he had nothing to do with it.

Traditionally the Treasurer is the last line of defence in this game. You are the miserable character who voices doubts and reservations because you have to write the cheque out. You have two weapons to fight with – bloody minded obstinacy and the business case. The control point is to make sure that you get the information to get a good decision taken.

A good decision is one that members do not accuse you of getting wrong for the next twenty years.

TIMETABLES AND CRITICAL PATHS

Decisions to buy things gather their own momentum. If fund raising is involved a head of steam builds up to buy the thing the money is being raised for. The longer and harder people work on an idea, the more eager they are to see it through whatever the cost. The danger is that mass hysteria takes over from logical judgement.

People's perceptions of time and speed vary too. A week, to someone holding down a responsible job with maybe one hour a night of true free time, seems no time at all. To a full-time officer with nothing but the voluntary organisation to think about, the week seems an age. When these two meet to discuss the project they may be speaking different languages.

It helps to map out at the start what you expect the project timetable to be. Spell out the information needed before you can even think about the decision. Agree checkpoints where you can assess progress. Agree who is responsible for getting things done and make sure they agree.

Assets

Just a couple of notes. This should not be the Treasurer's pigeon.

REGISTER

It helps to know what you own and where it is.

Make sure there is a register of all assets with details of

- date of purchase
- cost (estimate if donated)
- current value and replacement cost
- location

SECURITY

At a school event one night, the Treasurer walked off to collect her raffle prize, leaving the biscuit tin full of cash, unattended, on a table in the lobby. Video cameras are probably over the top, but at least think about how you can protect things that 'walk' easily.

Liabilities

THESE ARE OFTEN PEOPLE!

Hidden dangers

A reminder to read the small print in the contract so that you do not end up with liabilities you did not realise were there. *Watch* consumer protection programmes rather than appear on them as 'casualties'.

Principles Of Control

The principles of good control are:

More than one person
Independent check
Separation
Evidence
Rotation

That just about gives an acronym to remember them by – MISER.

I have tried to explain each of these through the chapter but here are a few more general recommendations.

INDEPENDENT CHECK

Choose an auditor who takes the job seriously and goes through the record with heavy boots and fine toothcomb rather than someone who has no real idea of what is required and just adds up the columns on the accounts you have prepared. If you can charm an experienced accountant into this job he can probably help with the design of your control systems too.

Make inspection and review of important items, like hall bookings or membership income, something that you do as a matter of course, even if infrequently. Knowing that someone else, who has a good knowledge of what should be going on, is going to review your records is a valuable deterrent. There is a fair chance of picking up honest mistakes in time to correct them too.

ROTATION

Encourage people to take on different tasks. Try not to let the same person do a job for more than a few years. Get someone to stand in and take over the job for holidays rather than leave it until the normal occupant comes back. Use rotas.

All these things reduce the risk of fraud. There is a much bigger benefit too. If the burden is carried by a few 'pillars' they become indispensable. Indispensable means a huge mess to clear up when they leave or die. If the same person runs the fête every year, and never trains a successor, the first fête after he leaves will be hard work. Spread the knowledge and the weight, use teams, train, develop talent. It has to be the best way.

A final stolen thought about pillars – they may hold the roof up but they also block out the view if you sit next to them and are almost impossible to move without bringing the whole house down.

3
THE CASH BOOK

Introduction

If you are looking after a small organisation with income below VAT registration limits, most, and maybe all, of your accounting work can be done with a simple, well laid out, cash book and a file of supporting vouchers. Two principles to follow are:

1. Make the lay-out of headings in the cash book as close to the shape of your final 'income and expenditure account' as possible.
2. Make sure that the figures you write down in the cash book can be followed through to the bank statement.

Before you dash out to buy the biggest and best bound book you can find, it is worth looking at what you actually need and what you want to do with it. 20 columns with space for the next 20 years is commendable, and probably works out the cheapest in cost per year; but will it go in your brief case, shopping bag or executive case for reference at meetings? I find an A4 cash book with around a dozen columns and 40 lines to the page provides enough detail for analysis of major headings. It also fits the briefcase and the bookshelf. One Treasurer I know uses two cash books and alternates year by year. That way she can give the auditor all last year's records and leave him to it.

You can put receipts and payments on facing pages. By tradition receipts go on the left and payments on the right. This has the advantage of keeping all the transactions in full view. It also leaves a lot of blank paper if the number of receipts and payments do not match. My experience is that it is easier to divide the book into two sections, one for receipts and one for payments. Look at the old cash book to gauge how much room to leave. Tape a tag at the front of each to show which is which. Otherwise you always open the book to the wrong one.

The amount of detail across the page is a personal decision but look first at the published accounts and, if you look after a 'branch' of a larger organisation, any analysis requirements that your 'head office' places on you.

This might be in the shape of a proforma return. You may decide that the information you want to keep needs more analysis than this requires, but it will make your life easier if your cash book design provides at least what the return asks for.

By separating receipts and payments you can use two facing pages as one extended page. This gives loads of columns for detail but keeps the size of the book down.

Payments

The layout of the first six columns might be as per figure 1:

Najafabad Community Hall Cash Book Payments (year)

1 Date	2 Payee & Description	3 Cheque No.	4 Ref.	5 Detail £	6 Bank £
....	....	......	.....	......	....

Figure 1 Example layout of the first six columns of Cash Book payments page

1. Date is the date which appears on the cheque.
2. Payee is the full name of the person or organisation who was paid. Description is to say what it was for and a brief reminder of anything unusual about the payment. Always assume future amnesia, and, if you have to make any calculations to work out what the payments should be, try to write them legibly and keep them on file. The note in the cash book might just read 'see calculation' or 'storm damage'. Believing that the thing is so unusual that you could never forget it will give you a headache ten months from now when you cannot remember. Good documentation is also a courtesy to the auditor and your successor.
3. Cheque number. The last three digits will be adequate. Where the payment is made by standing order or direct debit enter 'S.O.' or 'D.D.' in the cheque book number field. If the bank send you an advice form each time a payment is made this can be referenced up as you would an invoice. If not, do not bother to allocate a reference number.
4. Payment reference is the unique reference which you write on the paperwork that supports the payment. I use P/(yr)/1, P/(yr)/2, P/(yr)/3 and so on, where P stands for payment,

and 1 is the reference for the first payment in the year.

5. Detail. This column will not be used that often but, if the payment is made up of several similar items, backed up by a number of vouchers, this allows you to get the full story onto the face of the cash book, where it is easier to read than in the back-up.

Your club Secretary has just run four fund-raising events and put in his expense claim. His supporting vouchers are all in order and he has summarised his claim (see figure 2).

M Faraji Expenses

Jumble Sale 10/6/(year)	
Advertising: Najafabad Gazette	7.45
Refreshments: Ali Baba Superstores	21.00
	£28.45
Quiz Night 23/6/(year)	
Photocopying	12.50
Hire of P.A. system	25.00
Refreshments	15.60
	£53.10
Square Dance 4/7/(year)	
Tickets printing: 'Zootprint'	27.50
Caller fee	40.00
	£67.50
Stall at Charities Market 11/7/(year)	
Pitch fee	5.00
Coffee for helpers	1.15
	£6.15
Total reimbursement requested	**£155.20**

Figure 2 Expense claim

You want to record the costs of each event separately but he does not want four cheques, just one. Your options are:

a) a one line entry with a note to remind yourself to refer to the back-up for the full story.

b) use the 'detail' column (see figure 3).

Najafabad Community Hall Cash Book Payments (year)

1	2	3	4	5	6
Date	Payee & Description	Cheque No.	Ref.	Detail £	Bank £
....	....	......	.....	....	....
15/7/(yr)	M Faraji	201	45		
	Jumble Sale			28.45	
	Quiz Night			53.10	
	Square Dance			67.50	
	Charities Mkt			6.15	155.20

Figure 3 Cash Book entry of payment to Secretary for expenses

The 'detail' column lets you expand the entry without losing sight of the value of the cheque drawn.

6. Bank. The amount shown here is the value that will appear on the bank statement. When the 'detail' column is used it will be a sub-total.

If you are short of space, compress the date by leaving out the year – you have already written the year in big letters at the top of the page – and shorten the 'reference' to the number itself. So P/(yr)/45 written on the invoice would become simply '45' in the cash book.

ANALYSIS – THE COLUMNS TO THE RIGHT OF 'BANK'

The job of the first six columns is to record the essential facts. Beyond column 6 you are using the cash book to summarise the payments and receipts by type, a shorthand set of accounts. Your particular requirements take over. But, as a rule of thumb, at the far right leave four free columns. These are for:

1. Notes and scribbles.
2. Suspense.
3. Deposit transfers.
4. Sundry or miscellaneous.

If, occasionally, expense claims are made after deducting cash received you need another column headed 'receipts'.

1. Notes and scribbles

This is effectively your right margin and allows the auditor room to play as well as leaving you space to put big red asterisks (nearest thing to a knotted handkerchief) and cross references. Write notes here rather than in the analysis columns. Words distract your eye when you are trying to do or check the additions.

2. Suspense

More on this later, appropriately if you think about it.

3. Deposit transfers

Accounting for movements between current account and deposit account often causes confusion. Partly it is because common sense tells you that it is not really a payment and definitely not an expenditure. Remember that the 'cash book' for this purpose is synonymous with the current, or main, account. If you write a cheque on the current account to pay in to the building society, or ask the bank to transfer funds from the current account to deposit account, then you are taking money out of the current account and, as far as the current account goes, it counts as a payment. If you enter it in this column and refuse to panic it will work out.

4. Sundry or miscellaneous

Alias rag bag or 'I'm not quite sure which category this falls into'. If half your entries end up in sundry you have not worked out your requirements properly. It is not a synonym for 'small'. Sundry payments can be any size. You can also use it to highlight abnormal things. The members should not need to ask what is in sundry. You should show them. It is not for tucking away embarrassing payments. Neither does it mean 'slush fund'. Our new Najafabad Hall Treasurer decides that his main headings will be:

Equipment
Cleaning
Consumables
Repairs & maintenance
Light & heat
Rates & insurance

Last year the published accounts showed the analysis of expense as in figure 4.

Looking at the cash book for last year this was his reasoning.

Cleaning was a combination of wages and materials. Although below the level at which he would have to account for tax and national insurance, he wanted to focus on this as a distinct item. So he has split out the materials in the 'consumables' line.

Repairs and maintenance fluctuate from year to year, but are

Expenditure	**(last year)**	**(year before)**
Equipment	£ —	£ 497
Rates & water rates	245	210
Insurance	55	51
Telephone	85	157
Postage & stationery	106	—
Repairs & maintenance	81	223
Bank charges	1	5
Cleaning	617	365
Light & heat	82	—
Sundry	35	34
	£1307	£1542

Figure 4 Analysis of expense from published accounts

still important. Keep separate.

Light and heat had been paid direct by the local council until the end of last year. It was going to be increasingly important to keep individual focus on this area.

Rates and water rates were paid by standing order. Two entries each month suggested they should have their own column. The insurance was a single premium so he decided to put it in with rates to keep sundry clear. The areas he grouped together in sundry were:

Postage and stationery. Last year saw a one-off payment for leaflets which should not be needed this year.

Telephone. This should be four standard invoices. They had now had the phone 'adjusted' by BT so that it would only accept incoming and 'emergency' calls. This after it had proved impossible to identify and restrain 'private' use.

Bank charges. He had no intention of paying any if he could help it.

There are no absolute right or wrong answers to this question. Thinking about it helps, as does trying to understand why the last Treasurer did it the way he did.

The finished cash book payments page now looks like figure 5. It may help to draw a thick line down the page to the right of the Bank column. This reminds you that everything to the right of the line is analysis of the amounts shown on the left.

Najafabad Community Hall Cash Book Payments (year)

Date	Payee & Description	Chq No.	Ref.	Detail £	Bank £	Equip.	Clean	Cons	Rep & Maint	Light & Heat	Rates & Ins	Sndry	Trans-fers	Susp

Figure 5 Cash Book payments page

Receipts

The lay-out of the first five columns of the receipts page would be as shown in figure 6.

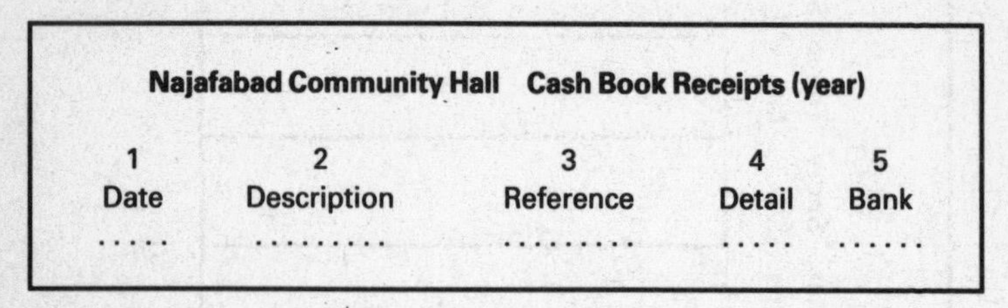

Najafabad Community Hall Cash Book Receipts (year)

1 Date	2 Description	3 Reference	4 Detail	5 Bank
.....	....	....	.....	......

Figure 6 First five columns of Cash Book receipts page

There are five columns rather than six because although banks do number pay-in slips they never seem to show the pay-in slip number on the bank statement where it would be really useful. But, do check your pay-in slips. If they have boxes for comments use them and write in your receipt's reference or some narrative. This will then appear on the bank statement.

1. Date is the date you pay the money into the bank.
2. Description should include whom it is from, what it is for and who gave it to you. For example – "members' subs, Mrs Pritchard".
3. Reference is to the back-up documentation. As with payments I use R/(yr)/1, R/(yr)/2, R/(yr)/3, and so on. The full reference is written onto the vouchers, the cash book entry can be abbreviated to the number alone.
4. Detail is even more important for receipts than for payment. Instead of being a useful method of breaking items down it is the only way to keep track of cash pay-ins on the bank statement.

   As an auditor it drives me mad to have to guess which entries in the cash book made up a composite entry on the bank statement. When it happens I also have to spend more time to be absolutely sure that nothing untoward is happening. The entries in 'detail' should sub-total to and tie up with the actual pay-in slip used so that you can tell instantly that all the cash has been credited to the account.

   If the bank does something peculiar, like crediting the cash and cheques as two individual values, make a note in the back-up file and on the face of the bank statement when you first sort it out. Remember, 'Always Assume Amnesia'.

5. Bank – covered above. A cash book which always shows in the bank column the amount that appears on the bank statement will have a much happier and less stressed auditor, which should mean that you keep him for longer.

ANALYSIS

At the far right, again leave four columns for:
1. Notes and scribbles.
2. Suspense.
3. Transfers from deposit (abbreviates to 'Trfrs').
4. Sundry or miscellaneous.

Suspense: I'm still keeping you in it.

Transfers From Deposit. Again, common sense tells you that this is not really a receipt because you have taken it off deposit and it is demonstrably not 'income' – you are only making the transfer because the account is short of cash. But it is, from the point of view of the current account, something which increases the balance. It is a receipt into the current account. Just enter it and stop worrying.

If you ever have to make payments from cash, if a visiting speaker or member reasonably wishes to be re-imbursed for out of pocket expenses in cash rather than by cheque, you will need an additional column entitled 'payments'. This would be entered in brackets or in red to remind you that it is a negative item.

For the main headings for receipts our Treasurer opts for:

Grants received	Donations
Membership subscriptions	Use of hall
Fund-raising	

These he took straight from last year's accounts.

Income	**(last year)**	**(year before)**
Grants received	£ 751	£ 320
Donations	–	6
Membership subs	17	20
Use of hall	800	682
Fund-raising	127	193
Deposit interest	8	–
Sundry	28	30
	£1731	£1251

Figure 7 Analysis of income

Notice that there is no column for deposit interest because that interest arises from and is credited to the deposit account.

For churches and other charities, donations would require more analysis. For example 'voluntary giving' could be split into:

Planned giving
- covenanted
- not covenanted

Unplanned

The approach again is to try to get onto the face of the cash book the headings that will give you the most informative 'at a glance' picture of what is happening and enable you to prepare reports quickly.

Our Najafabad Hall receipts page now looks like figure 8.

Suspense

One of my Treasurer friends used to title this 'ins and outs'. Consider some examples of what would go into the suspense account.

1. If you take up a collection or whip round for a worthy cause, but something other than the club or association itself – say a visiting speaker represents a charity – then the collection is not strictly the income of the club, and paying the money over is not the club's expenditure. Enter both collection cash and the subsequent payment in 'suspense'.
2. Deposits collected by you for the use of the hall and returned in full only after the caretaker confirms that there are no problems. The deposit is not income but money held which belongs to someone else. Both the deposit receipt and the re-payment go into 'suspense'. If you were to include the deposits received as hall income and their return as hall expense you would be overstating the amounts, perhaps considerably.
3. Deposits paid by you for use of an outside facility or to hire equipment and later returned.
4. Floats drawn for jumble sales or fêtes and paid back into the bank with the take.

In all these cases there is neither genuine income nor expense. In time all the payments and receipts will come out to zero. The spirit of the suspense account is:

If you have received it you are going to have to pay it out.
If you have paid it you are going to get it back.

You can also use 'suspense' as a holding column for unexplained items on the bank statement. In fact, if you are

Najafabad Community Hall Cash Book Receipts (year)

Date	Description	Ref.	Detail £	Bank £	Grants	Dons	Memb Subs	Use of Hall	Fund Raise	Sndry	Trfr Dep	Susp	

Figure 8 Cash Book receipts page

completely unsure where to put something, use suspense.

This makes it doubly important to keep the account under control, and to 'clear the bucket' regularly.

Over time the theory is that the payments and receipts will match exactly. At any one time there may be items outstanding on both sides. A 'suspense control log' can help, as shown in figure 9.

Suspense Control Log

Paid		Received	
1/1/(yr) Deposit for hire of French polishing machine	£20.00	30/1/(yr) Collection for Salv'n Army	£34.56
		10/2/(yr) Bank entry unexplained	45.00
28/2/(yr) Salvation Army	34.56		
1/3/(yr) Jumble Sale float (Mrs Jenkins)	£50.00		
	£104.56		£79.56

Figure 9 Example of a suspense control log

The balance on suspense, the difference between payments and receipts, is £25. More importantly it is made up of 3 items which you can identify as not yet zeroing off. Keeping the log acts as a reminder that you still have not clarified the bank entry or got the deposit back. The idea of using suspense to record 'ins and outs' is so that you can keep track of them and not bloat up your accounts with entries that are not real income or expenditure of the organisation.

Net Items

How do you record cases where either:

a) someone is handing over an amount of cash after deducting his, or several people's, expenses?

b) the cash is being counted and someone needs a reimbursement for which a cheque would be inappropriate? (E.g. they do not have a bank account.)
c) the club agreed to pay the net cost of a coach trip to help keep the individual ticket price down?

The basic principles are:
- the entry in the cash book should be for the same value as will appear in the bank statement.
- tell the full story, show both sides.

Example a. The Secretary ran a raffle for a donated bottle of whisky.
50 tickets at 50p each.
The gross take was £25.00 but he had to buy a book of tickets for £1.98.
That leaves you with a net cash amount to pay in of £23.02.

METHOD

1. In the narrative section make entries as shown in figure 10.

1 Date	2 Description	3 Reference	4 Detail £	5 Bank £
.....	....	....	.....	......
1/3/(yr)	Raffle (M Faraji) (£25 less tickets)	47		23.02

Figure 10 Entries in narrative section

2. In the analysis section make entries as shown in figure 11.

6 Grants	7 Dons	8 Subs	9 Use of Hall	10 Fund Rais	11 Sndry	12 Depst	13 Susp	14 Paymts
.....	....	....	.....	....	....	....	....	.....
				25.00				(1.98)

Figure 11 Entries in analysis section

The analysis adds up to £23.02, but you keep track of the amounts paid out as well as the net.

Example b. The organiser might ask for re-imbursement of £35 because the coach cost £235 to hire and the ticket price was set at £5 for a 40 seater. You could enter the £35 and show the narrative as 'net cost of coach trip'. Better to show, in the analysis section, £235 in 'sundry' and (£200) in 'receipts'.

Bank Reconciliation

Each month, when you receive the bank statement, you should check it and prepare a bank reconciliation. The purposes are:

1. Pick up bank errors.
2. Make sure all the money you have paid in has actually been credited to the account.
3. Identify cheques not yet presented.
4. Check the balance in hand after everything has gone through.
5. Make sure you pick up mistakes early.

Starting from the cash book, mark off each item on the bank statement. A coloured pencil or pen helps. Change the colour each month so that you do not confuse last month's ticks with this month's. Where you cannot find the corresponding entry on the bank statement note the cash book with 'o/s' or some other small tidy note to show that it is outstanding. Make your ticks small and do not disfigure either the bank statement or the cash book to the extent that you cannot read the original entries.

Where there is an entry on the bank statement that you recognise and agree but is not yet entered in the cash book, write it up using the date given on the bank statement. This would include standing orders and direct debits, but do be sure you really understand what they are before entering them.

When the cash book is up to date for everything you recognise you can prepare the formal reconciliation. Another phrase for 'bank reconciliation' would be 'how much is there really in the bank?'.

First work out the balance in hand or overdrawn according to the cash book. This is the amount that your cash book tells you is in the bank or overdrawn if only the bank had put everything through.

If you are using separate pages for payments and receipts there is no need to keep writing in a formal balance through the year.

The first entry in the cash book for the period should be the balance brought forward. If there is a balance of cash at the bank it will be brought forward on the receipts pages. If the balance is overdrawn it will be brought forward on the payments page.

As you enter the payments and receipts for the year keep a running total of payments and receipts, including the brought forward. Take payments away from receipts and you have your current balance.

I usually update the running totals in pencil each time I enter up the cash book and calculate the balance, noting it at the side of the page with the date. It is a good and quick way of making sure you do not go overdrawn unintentionally.

Next head up a sheet of paper and start with the balance according to the bank:

Najafabad C.H. National Bank current account 136573
Bank Reconciliation at 1st April (year)

Balance per bank at 30th March (year) £1292.23

(List all the items where cash has been paid in but the bank does not yet show it on the statement.)

Add: Bankings not yet credited, paid in 31/3/(yr) 250.00

(Then list all the cheques which you have marked 'o/s' in the cash book because they have not yet appeared on a statement.)

Less: Cheques not yet presented

3467	24/3	23.67	
3468	24/3	14.12	
3469	25/3	257.46	
			(295.25)
			£1246.98

(If you are lucky, the figure you have got down to now is the same figure as you have already worked out from the cash book. But not always. If the bank has a payment showing on the bank statement that you have not got in the cash book it will make the 'bank' figure a lower balance or a bigger overdraft

than your 'cash book' figure, so you have to add it on. If the bank has a receipt on the bank statement that you do not have in the cash book it will make the bank balance higher or the overdraft lower, so you have to deduct it.)

(You are not making a philosophical statement, just writing down all the reasons why the two figures are not the same. Look through the bank statement for items which are not ticked because they do not appear in the cash book.)

Add:	payments on bank statement not in cash book	25.00
Less:	receipts on bank statement not in cash book	450.00
Balance per cash book 1/4/(yr)		£821.98

(If, after all this, the balance you have got to is not the balance you have worked out from the cash book, go to the next section (below).

Just to make sure I have the right figures I usually write a note at the bottom of the page, showing where the cash book figure came from.)

Balance brought forward 1/1/(yr)	356.26
Add total receipts	2456.03
	2812.29
Less total payments	(1990.31)
Balance per cash book	£821.98

BUT WHAT WHEN IT DOESN'T BALANCE?

The whole point of doing the 'bank rec' is to pick up problems. The fun starts when the reconciliation does not reconcile.

Look first at the last reconciliation. Have all the cheques shown there as outstanding cleared yet? Did you include them on your list this time?

Scan cash book and bank statements for items not ticked. Check the additions in the cash book.

Make sure you are not missing a page of the bank statement and that the balances carried forward at the end of one statement are the same as those at the start of the next.

Make sure it is your bank statement.

See if the difference divides by nine. It could be a transposition error. If you write down the right numbers in the

wrong order, not an unusual mistake, by some magic the difference does divide by nine.
569 recorded as 596 – difference 27
123 recorded as 321 – difference 198
1327 recorded as 1732 – difference 405

It also works if you have missed a zero off the end but that one is easier to spot.

Check the cash book to see if you are working with the pages for this year. Now do the same with the bank statement.

Look at cheque stubs – have you entered all of them in the cash book?

Let someone else have a look at it. You have probably stared your mistake square in the face six times, but it was your brain that made it to start with and it is a consistent creature – it keeps on making it.

Interesting items thrown up by my bank recs have included:

* a cheque drawn on someone else's account
* cash deposits belonging to someone else with a similar account number
* previously cancelled direct debits

WHAT NEXT?

The reconciliation now gives you a list of the items which cause the bank statement to show a different amount from the cash book. If this was hard work there is a great temptation to sign and date the reconciliation with a flourish and make a coffee. I do recommend that you sign and date it, but you should also go on from there to review any actions you need to take.

Monies Paid in But Not Yet Credited by the Bank

How long is the delay? Two or three days is not unusual. Cash paid in on the 22nd of the month might well come up on the bank statement on the 23rd, 24th or 25th. Who paid the money in? If you have regular long gaps you ought to find out why. The auditor should want to know the reasons anyway. If it is a large amount that is outstanding, check with the bank. They could have credited it to someone else's account.

Cheques Not Yet Presented

Be realistic. If you put it in the post second class the week before the statement date the payee may not even have it yet.

Concentrate particularly on any cheque which is outstanding two months running. Action depends on circumstances. It could be a gentle reminder to the Chairman to pay his expenses cheque in. Phone the insurance company, gas board or BT to stop supplies being withdrawn or cover lapsing.

Sometimes just wait and see. The important point is to ask yourself what the consequences are if the cheque has not reached its intended destination.

If you establish that the cheque has gone astray, contact the bank to stop the original cheque and draw another. Consider sending the replacement by registered mail.

Items on Bank Statement Not in Cash Book

I mean here the ones you do not understand. Contact the bank and ask them to send you copies of the paperwork they hold to support the entry. Ignore completely the narrative on the statement. On one occasion I rang in haste because we appeared to have been credited with someone's 'SALARY'. I had visions of some poor devil finding his mortgage not paid. The paperwork was for a quarterly dividend payment, which did belong to us. Another one was a 'COUNTER CREDIT'. 'Can you tell me,' I asked, 'What the charge made to our account on 14th March, entitled 'Counter credit' was?'. Quick as a flash the bank employee replied, 'Well, it's a counter credit'. It turned out to be cash, drawn in the bank, against our account, by someone who was not a signatory.

If a bank error, or unreasonable delay in crediting cash, gives rise to charges, complain. The 'counter credit' incident resulted in a £20 donation to the church. Well reasoned and justifiable complaints will often result in a reversal of charges.

Use the bank reconciliation itself to note the results of any enquiries. Keep all your old reconciliations on file.

Ruling Off and Checking Additions

Cash books are like string; leave them to their own devices and they get tangled up. Depending on the number of entries, consider ruling off the cash book either monthly or quarterly. Check that the totals of all the columns to the right of 'bank' add up to the same figure that the bank column does. The only difference will be the year's brought forward balance. That is in the 'bank' column but nowhere else.

If the bank reconciliation works out, the problem will be in the analysis section. Look first to see if you have entered every payment and receipt. Then go for the differences divisible by 9 again. Quickest by far is to ask someone else to take a look. Put the sub-totals in by pencil and go over with a pen when you have sorted any problems out. Leave a couple of lines blank before you resume.

Computerisation

The great thing about computers is that they do their own additions. There is nothing in the cash book design given above that cannot be done with a spreadsheet model, or with a bespoke accounts package. The 'suspense control' sheet works brilliantly on spreadsheet and there are few restrictions on the number of analysis columns you can use. Using a PC may even mean that the first great lie – 'It will only take you a few hours a month' comes true.

But there are safeguards to consider if you computerise.

AUDIT TRAIL

Bespoke accounting packages should provide complete records of all your entries and have controls built into them. They may be certified by one of the Accountancy Institutes. This quality will be built into the price. It also usually requires education and maintenance.

If you opt for a cheap and cheerful solution, at least get your auditor to take a look before you go live. Consider keeping manual and computer records side by side while you discover and sort out gremlins.

Manual cash books do not allow you to re-write history. Computers sometimes do. Make sure there is a discipline built in to stop you pressing the wrong button and wiping the year's records.

DISASTER RECOVERY

This posh term invites you to consider what would happen if your computer blew up, was dropped during redecorating, had coffee spilt in its innards, became gunged up by a virus on one of the games the children 'borrowed' from a friend, or any other calamity you like to think of.

You should have a routine for keeping back-up copies on diskettes, both of the transactions and of the programmes you run on. Old hat stuff this. Now, if you do have a PC, ask yourself whether you have all your essential programmes and data backed up.

It is a good idea to print out the records at each update and store a copy for safe-keeping.

Think about how you would manage if your PC does go on the blink. A friend with a compatible model? Manual records?

This problem is not unique to computers. Perhaps you could consider taking copies of the cash book pages to file in a safe place in case of a disaster striking the cash book – like leaving it on the bus or tube.

LICENCE FEE

A software licence may not be legally transferable from one PC to another without further payment. You should certainly check with the supplier beforehand as to what will happen when you resign and hand over to someone else.

Another option is to keep the manual cash book for the basic records – the left hand section up to bank – and use a spreadsheet to do the analysis. It means slightly more work to record the key information twice but gives the speed and flexibility to produce reports, budget projections and 'what if' cases when needed.

If you use a PC anyway you do not need telling about productivity and benefits. Computerise the process by all means. First design the lay-out and information requirements set out earlier in the chapter and make sure you understand and can meet them. There must be a record which lists the payments and receipts in date order, referenced to cheque numbers and other supporting documentation. That record must be capable of being audited. Think too of your successor. You have no right to assume or dictate that he or she will be computer literate.

Know how to 're-manualise' if you have to.

If you have never used a PC before it would be ambitious to try to become a user through computerising your accounts. Ambitious not impossible. Even a very simple spreadsheet model can literally reduce effort by half or more. Learn to use the beast generally first. Then look at using it for this particular task.

Your auditor is entitled to know of fundamental changes like computerisation in advance. He may also be able to help. Consult him.

Supporting Records

VOUCHERS

I want to introduce a technical term here – 'voucher'. It is a useful term for any piece of paper which is evidence for what you are paying or receiving. It can be an invoice from a supplier, a letter from a member, an architect's certificate, a pay-in slip. Almost all of your payments and receipts should have a 'voucher' of some sort to support them. They are your 'supporting records'.

As an auditor the sight of a brown envelope and the words 'You'll find everything in here' cause severe depression. Everything that is in there may well be there, but not referenced and not in the right order. Then there is the guessing game of which entries do not have anything to support them. Make life easy for yourself, your auditor and your successor. Have a filing system. A lever arch folder, a set of cardboard dividers and a hole punch provide the basics.

Sections I have found convenient are:

1. Invoices not yet paid.
2. Bank reconciliations.
3. Bank statements.
4. Bank correspondence.
5. Other correspondence, suppliers' statements etc.
6. Receipt vouchers.
7. Payment (or expense) vouchers.
8. Bank authorities for standing orders and direct debits.
9. Bank mandates.

At the end of each year these are transferred to a separate file, along with the working papers and the final accounts, and labelled up so that they can be stored for future reference.

It is usually easier to file old to the bottom and new to the top. You may choose to use more than one file but there are benefits to keeping all the vouchers together in one place, like knowing that what you are looking for must be there and not worrying in case something found its way into the rubbish sack.

File all vouchers as soon as possible, even if only to punch them and stick them in section 1. When you enter the cash book, allocate the reference and write it clearly on the voucher. Write the date paid and the cheque number on payments vouchers. It stops you paying them twice.

If the bill is small and flimsy – the infamous till roll – stick it onto a stout piece of paper so that it will not go walkabout, and so that the content is visible without dismantling the whole file. If several similar scraps of paper make up the evidence for a payment, summarise the information at the time you pay and attach the back up in the same order as on the summary. If you tame the scraps of paper when you first deal with them they will behave next time too.

When you are asked to make payment without evidence to support it do think about whether that is reasonable. A brief signed note from the person asking for the money is worth more than a till roll for the week's groceries with items circled in red. A receipt for postage stamps tells you no more than the fact that someone bought postage stamps. A notebook showing what the letters were for is better. If there is no voucher, write a note which explains why there is none and consider getting the payment minuted. Invoices do get lost, especially if they are for small values.

Be reasonable about what evidence you demand but also firm in saying that evidence should be produced when you believe that to be the case. If the individual managed to get the money without your approval, present him with a note to sign for your records, confirming what happened.

The end result should be a file of supporting records which are a joy to audit and simple to refer to when questions arise.

4
CHANGING YOUR BANK ACCOUNT

Why Change?

A bank manager who is supportive of what you are doing is a treasure, but bank managers move on and so do head office policies. Keep the service provided under review. It is not only a question of the best deposit rate and lowest charges. Opening hours, accessibility, night safe facilities and efficiency, length of queues at the times you want to pay money in, all count. How easy is the bank to get to? How responsive are they to your needs? Do you get personal attention, like a phone call to warn you that you need to transfer money from deposit rather than an important cheque being bounced? The value of the total service to you is more than the naked arithmetic of the interest rates.

Do not restrict the review to high street banks – building societies and Girobank may well be competitive choices.

Early Steps

SIGNAL

Let the other members of the committee know that you are actively contemplating change – they may have good ideas. Request a list from your bank of:

a) direct debit instructions
b) standing orders
c) valuables in safe-keeping
d) all other accounts in the club/association name with details of balances in hand.

(The last because it does sometimes happen that special accounts get opened, forgotten and left to accumulate interest with the statements being faithfully sent to the originating Treasurer.)

This also gives the bank manager a chance to offer improved

terms if he wants to keep the account.

AUTHORISATION

Present a formal recommendation to the committee which gives you the authority to open the new accounts, close the old ones, names the cheque signatories and requests the old bank to deliver items in safe-keeping.

Plan the Change-over

Open the new bank account with a minimum balance. Work out the next three months' cash movements in detail. In particular, list out the dates and amounts of all standing orders and direct debits and the expected dates and amounts of any dividend or investment income. Every single payment or receipt that goes automatically to the old account has to be changed so that it will feed the new one. At the same time you need to manage the balance on both accounts so that neither incurs avoidable bank charges. If you have spare cash on deposit, it may be worth moving some into the two current accounts for the change-over period, to reduce the risk of either going overdrawn. Whatever you do, do not close the old account yet.

Confirm the Basis of the New Account

Ask the bank to confirm the status and terms of the new account in writing. That includes registering it to receive interest gross if applicable. It would be a pity to go to all this trouble and then lose a quarter's interest because the bank set up the new account wrongly.

Set Up a Control Schedule for Standing Payments

This would be a separate list for each type of item. Across the page you would have columns for:

Name
Amount & frequency
Instruction sent
Instruction acknowledged
Cleared from old account
Appears on new account

Your old and new bank may be able to make the changes for you. Ask them how they would prefer the transfer to be handled. As each stage is complete for each item, write in the date completed. Review the control sheet for gaps and chase up with phone calls and letters. Experience is that at least one will go wrong, perhaps more. By keeping a clear schedule you can tell at a glance how things are going.

Outstanding Cheques

Use the latest bank reconciliation as another tracking sheet and mark off cheques as they clear. One of the most common mistakes is to close the old bank account with cheques still outstanding. When they are paid in, they bounce, cause embarrassment to you, involve new cheques, letters of apology and legitimate charges from the old bank.

Income

Set up a control schedule listing all the sources of income. Send letters informing everyone that needs to know about the change. Payments all originate from one place – you. Income can involve many different people. It is not unusual for organisations to carry on paying money into the same account in spite of several letters. If you have a lot of people contributing donations or subscriptions by standing order this can be a big job. It also needs tact – they are being asked to take trouble for your benefit, so they deserve a considered (but not libellous) explanation of the change.

In the Cash Book

Start a new page for the new account. Continue to enter the old page for the old account. Do not try to write up the entries for both accounts on the same page – you may know what you are doing when you start but, even a month on, you will get horribly confused. Transfers between the accounts can be put in the transfers to and from deposit column with a note to remind you which account it was. Alternatively, if you have a spare column, use it.

Wait

When you are sure that every cheque has cleared, that every direct debit or standing order is being actioned on the new account, that income is also going to the right account, wait. Transfer all but a small, no charges, balance to the new account and leave the old account alone. Unless you are in serious need of the money (the holding balance may only be £50) leave the old account open until a few clear statements confirm that all is in order.

Close the Old Account

Finally, close the old account and hope that the new account will not need to be changed for a long time.

5
PLANNING

What is a Plan?

Planning is about survival, coping with change, development, achieving basic aims, and budgets. Budgets are important, but before rushing in to the 'how to' of working them out, it is worth thinking about the framework you use them in, the plan process itself.

The purpose of a plan is to provide a structure, or a map, to work out where you will end up if you carry on the same way, so that you can work out where you really want to go and how to get there, and to carry everyone along with you.

It is an organised and creative way of thinking ahead and taking decisions. Every individual or organisation is affected by a combination of external factors and their own choices. The external factors can be history, place, genetics, how much you inherited, educational and social background, the site of the clubhouse, the County structure plan, village population, or current membership numbers. If you were to plot the last year's actual financial results and add in some guesses on inflation and new prices – subscriptions, lettings rates – you would be charting, to a large extent, a picture which represents all those external factors.

A good plan comes in where this picture stops. You start with a 'no change' view. Add to it a vision of where you want to go, risks involved, actions required, things that have to be changed, the timescale, and who is responsible for making each action happen. That is a plan. It is far too important to be left to the Treasurer.

Is There a Plan Process?

What happens today? If anything?

APPARENT CHAOS

No budgets or financial forecasts are prepared. Neither Chairman nor committee members see anything to do with finances, other than the annual accounts, which they do not try to understand anyway. This method can work very effectively as long as the Treasurer knows what is going on at all times and is competent. It certainly avoids the 'if there's a budget why don't we spend it' mentality as there is no budget to spend. However, it places much of the decision process with the Treasurer – if he does not like an idea he says there is no money for it – and not with the committee or the wider membership. This is not wrong; it ought, though, to be the way that the membership chooses to operate rather than one they are forced to put up with.

As Treasurer, if you work this way, you carry the entire can all on your own.

BUDGET & CONTROL CYCLE

Financial forecasts are prepared on a regular, probably annual, basis. Financial estimates are made for areas like fund-raising, maintenance costs and lettings income. The overall figures are converted into budgets which are given out to the people responsible. At its simplest level the choir are told how much they can spend on new and replacement music and the Sunday School on training materials and handbooks.

Either monthly or quarterly what has actually happened is compared with the plan, and actions are worked out to deal with problems. This is very much the normal business method. It tends to look at figures which can be estimated from past history. This process is thoroughly responsible, can be democratic, and should ensure that the financial affairs are properly conducted with plenty of early warning of problems.

It can also be a treadmill which is very hard to look up from. Budgets tend to be based on what happened last year. The priorities in the past shape the future and people get into the habit of using the money, without challenging whether it is the right amount for today's needs.

STRATEGIC PLAN

The previous models can and do work effectively. The difference between them and the strategic plan is the breathing space for radical and creative thought along the lines of:

What are we here for?
What do we want to achieve?
How can we achieve it?
What stands in the way?
What are we forced to do?

What are we going to do about it?

What are we here for?

This does not have to be complex to be effective. It can be a simple statement.

To play cricket.

To play cricket in a friendly atmosphere.

To play cricket at senior club level.

To play cricket and to provide training and encouragement to youngsters coming into the game.

It could be that the members are able to come up with a sentence that answers this question in five minutes.

Another description of this is 'Mission Statement'. This will cause automatic groans from some, especially those who have been battered into conversion at work. Even if the national body already has a mission statement in place there is room to discuss the style in which you go after it.

What do we want to achieve?

Size of membership.
Level of fund-raising.
League position and membership.
Increase in local awareness.
New strip for the youth team.
New building or equipment.

Usually these objectives flood from the discussion of the basic purpose. The brainstorm approach – where you write all the ideas up, however crazy – works. Think long term as well as this year. If there is a mountain to climb in the future consider it now.

How can we achieve it?

Who have we got and what can they do? What are the priorities? If we raise as much money as last year, how many of our priorities will be taken care of? What else can we do?

At the simplest level a small branch of a charity might set itself a target of £500 fund-raising and decide on two jumble sales, a quiz and a coffee morning, as the means by which to raise it. If they decide to double the fund-raising target they might look at a street collection or house-to-house collection. They might also re-visit their target membership numbers. Matching the objectives and the available resources is an area for special attention from the Treasurer. This could be the starting point for developing the budget.

St Raphael's Church Draft Plan for next year

£ Thousands	Last Yr	This Yr	Next Yr
Income before fund-raising			
Stewardship	4.1	4.5	4.5
Tax refunds	0.5	1.4	1.1
Collections	1.6	1.4	1.4
Investment income	0.7	0.8	0.6
Other	0.3	0.4	0.4
Parish Room surplus	0.5	—	—
	7.7	8.5	8.0
Expense before equipment			
Quota	4.6	5.0	6.2
Parish	1.7	1.8	2.0
Other			
Running	0.9	0.7	0.7
Worship	0.5	0.5	0.5
Office	0.1	0.2	0.2
Heat & light	0.6	0.6	0.7
Insurance	0.2	0.2	0.2
Gifts & gratuities	0.2	0.1	0.1
Misc	0.4	0.1	0.2
Total other	2.9	2.4	2.6
Total expense	9.2	9.2	10.8
Deficit (before fund-raising & equipment)	(1.5)	(0.7)	(2.8)
Equipment	(0.4)	(0.3)	
Deficit (after equipment & before fund-raising)	(1.9)	(1.0)	(2.8)
Fund-raising	1.9	1.5	
Surplus/Deficit	—	0.5	(2.8)

Figure 12 Example draft plan

This plan states a problem. If things continue as expected there will be a large deficit next year. In the past the gap has been covered by fund-raising, but next year the gap is much bigger. The other issue is a long list of equipment that various people would like to buy. The two main areas for decision are on equipment and the fund-raising activities, so these are highlighted separately to give them focus.

At least the problem is quantified. Any spend on equipment makes the forecast deficit bigger. The plan should be an agenda for action, a tool which prompts for decisions, not an academic exercise. It is also an opportunity to invite action and solutions from the wider body of members, and to take them up on their ideas.

What stands in the way?

The answer is a list of things that need changing. (I asked this in one lecture. A voice from the bottom of the table sighed, 'Only the Head and the Board of Governors.') First time round the suggestions will be anything **someone else** is responsible for. Keep off generalities: listing out apathy of the membership, lack of new blood on the committee, the Chairman and the Rector will not get you far. To avoid the grouse list, try picturing the ideal, the way you would really like things to be. Now, what would have to change to bring that about?

Go for specifics:

Arrangement of space in the clubhouse.
Improved facilities, say which ones.
Control over Church Hall bookings.
Membership numbers.

Sometimes the answers can be glaringly simple. Remember though, the Treasurer is not the one who has to come up with them. You are providing factual input to open up the discussion and to get the benefit of other people's involvement.

What are we forced to do?

This brings us back to external factors. It is worth building into the plan two basic checks:

1. Are there any changes in the law which we have to respond to? For example, in the past changes in trading law have affected the sale of second-hand electrical equipment and children's toys. Health and safety laws have required drastic improvement to kitchens and formal training in hygiene. Involving the wider membership pays off in this respect as you are more likely to identify the problems early.
2. Does what we are planning to do take us into new areas

where we will be caught by legislation that has not affected us so far?
VAT registration limits.
Income tax.

What are we going to do about it?

You still have to deal with the gap between what you want to do and the wherewithal you can see to do it. At this point you have to get over the cynicism of the experienced – all the people who knew all along that this fancy plan business would only end up telling you what they knew already, that there wasn't enough money for the normal things, never mind new ideas. The gap can be bridged by spending less or finding more. There are no magic answers. What can be magical is the way people achieve things when they have a say in the decisions.

Your job is to make clear the financial facts as you see them. Their job is to take decisions as to what the priorities are and how they will be met.

Whenever I get to this final stage of a plan I find myself torn into two different people: the plan co-ordinator who wants to reach for the moon and the financial realist who is very nervous about what can really be achieved. One way of handling this is to be two people – get someone else to own and run the plan in the first place, or get an outsider to review it.

Doing the Numbers – Practical Planning

Whichever approach you adopt, you need to prepare basic information. Take the last two or three years' accounts and pick out the separate activities which make up the income and expenditure. If you did this work at handover you are already in shape. If not, start now.

For each item prepare a schedule that sets out all the information and assumptions in plain English and simple arithmetic (see figures 13 and 14).

PRACTICAL POINTS ON THE SCHEDULES

The format of the schedules will vary according to the subject to be covered. You can add in percentage increase figures if you think it relevant. If you write down the reasons behind your estimate, it will make it easier for other people to understand and comment on the plan. The simpler the better – your target is not to mystify but to explain. Try to be open and not defensive when you take people through the figures. You want others, who may have special knowledge or a valuably different

Current Year Plan Working Schedule 1

Main fund-raising event

2 years ago Gift Day	£1426 net
Included sale of goods and refreshments approx. £200. No significant expenses. Members only.	
Last year Fête & Flower Festival	£1639 net
Fête was low key. Games and items for sale, refreshments. No Public Address system hired. No bands, displays, etc. Advertising £7 for local paper and home produced posters. Could just as easily have been an autumn or winter fair. Flower festival underwritten by Council. It cost them approx £500 and proceeds were only £250. Excellent weather and reasonable turn-out, despite several other events on same day.	
Current year Estimates	
Summer fête without flower festival	£1400
Gift Day	£1400

Other ideas to consider:
Increase scale of fête
Autumn fair? Christmas Bazaar?
Actions required:
Agree nature of event
Book dates in the diary
Appoint organiser

Figure 13

point of view, to test your assumptions, and tell you if they think something is wrong. Your aim is also involvement in the decisions. Steamroller a plan through aggressively and it will be your plan – you are on your own. Get the others involved in the thinking and the judgements and it is a shared idea that everyone pulls together to make succeed.

Good schedules also help when you come to explain why the estimates were out. Plans are never right; the world and events keep changing. They need to be revised and corrected, but measuring against them will give you a much better feel of trend and direction than having nothing to compare with.

Full year figures have a nasty habit of concealing big changes.

Current Year Plan Working Schedule 2

Heat & Light	Previous Year	Last Year	Current Year
Gas	358	741	729
Electricity	261	371	380

Notes: New extension completed Jan last yr. Previous year was slightly low because the building was out of action for the last two months. Main increase is from the new gas central heating system. First three months thermostat was set far too high and kept on too long. There were no price increases in the year.

Assumptions: No change in usage patterns

Price rise estimates for this year. Assume 5% at mid yr.

Calculation:

Gas	Base	£741
	Adjustment for resetting thermostat (Rough difference between 1Q and 4Q bills.)	(30)
		711
	Inflation 5% on half the year equals 2.5% overall	18
	Current estimate	729
Electricity	Base	371
	Inflation 2.5%	9
	Current estimate	380

Actions

* Review usage pattern with hall secretary. Any big changes since last discussion?
* Consider price rise to cover heat & light increases and pay for the improvement in the facilities.
* Monitor first quarter invoice to ensure no major variances.

Figure 14

Averages can be dangerous. 'A trend's a trend until it bends.' The heat and light calculation above looks authoritative but the word 'base' could be misleading.

Take these quarterly spends:

March	100
June	50
September	80
December	141
Full year	371

They could mean you are seeing a 40% plus increase in the second half of the year. September is a summer quarter up by £30 over June. December is up £41 over March. Try to sort out the facts before you jump to an answer. Make sure the first three bills were not estimates.

Think about the best way to analyse the data. For a church, you may get a better idea of trends by looking at a graph of the weekly collections than by looking just at the full year figure.

Economists can look at data big enough to be statistically reliable. They still get the answer wrong. For small figures it is important to make the calculations as factual as possible. Do not theorise or extrapolate figures if you can look at a list of facts. Estimating the tax refund for next year by looking at last year's total and adding on a percentage is inexcusable. Get the Stewardship Secretary to calculate the expected figure from his current records. Then make a judgement on likely changes and their impact. Do your homework.

PLANNING FOR DISASTERS

Each year seems to have its own unique and unplannable disaster. Murphy's law of planning is that you should always forecast at least one unknown problem. There will also be one area at least where the budget will not stretch. There are several ways of building in the flexibility to deal with these risks.

1. The honest way

Put a separate line in the expense budget labelled 'Contingency' at a value equal to the average of the last four years' unexpected item.

2. Slightly devious

Use the word 'say' on your worksheets. Whatever the detailed calculation comes out, round it up at the bottom – £235 = 'say' £250.

3. Devious

Build in the rounding to each stage of the calculation. Inflation or expected price increase of 3.2% becomes 4%. Last year's actual, the 'base', is rounded up.

Both 2 and 3 build in a level of safety but can also mean that you lose track of the right figure and allow expenses to creep up uncontrolled.

4. Consensus

Ask the people who are going to spend the money to work out what they need. Review all the requests in committee as a team and decide your priorities together.

Which approach you use will depend on your preference and the personalities involved.

Planning – the Treasurer's Role

What should the Treasurer's role be in the plan debate? I have never thought that Treasurers should set policy. I believe they should ensure that the calculations are rigorous and realistic. They should give everyone concerned a hard time until they are convinced that the facts stated are as right as they can be and show the financial consequences of decisions taken.

CASE STUDY

Your church building is tiny. Each year you just about scrape by. The vicar wants to extend the church and re-equip it. The total project cost is £110,000. The diocese will give you a grant of £90,000 but that leaves you with £10,000 for the building, and another £10,000 for equipment, still to find. The church owns investments of £10,000. Your annual outgoings and income are just about balanced at £8,000 per year. Now is the ideal time to do the building because costs are low. Wait and they could escalate out of reach. The proposal you are asked to consider is that the investments be sold and a commercial loan taken out to finance the project. There is no track record of large scale fund-raising. What would you recommend?

What actually happened?

The Treasurer's ordinary budget for the year in question showed a small deficit. The position given to the committee was that shown in figure 15.

My recommendation was not to go ahead **until** further assistance could be obtained. The impact of the proposals was huge in proportion to the normal budget. The committee accepted the analysis and went after more help. They managed to get a further grant and an interest free loan for the equipment. Three years on, their investments are intact and the loan is all but paid off, even if they are all sick and tired of raising money.

Running a Plan

One technique that can work is an open seminar. Put the

Expected normal income	£8000
Expense including known increases	8200
Deficit before project	(200)
Loss of income if investments sold (1)	(850)
Additional annual interest on loan (2)	(1500)
Deficit after impacts and before loan capital repayments	(2550)

Notes

1. Selling the investments to provide half the required cost would reduce income by approx £850 per year.
2. Paying interest on a commercial loan would be a further cash outflow. 15% assumed on an interest only basis.

Figure 15 Outline of financial position

committee or members into small working groups. Then write several questions on a flip chart and allocate them to the groups. Allow 20 minutes for discussion. Then feed back from the groups to the main forum. Limit the feedback to a 2 minute summary with the essence written on a flip chart. Stick the flip charts around the room as the meeting progresses. With six or so people in each group everyone gets a chance to put their ideas across and to be heard. The approach tends to unlock enthusiasm, and you find out what people actually think and believe. It also generates a sense of ownership of the actions that arise from the discussion.

Take the questions in order. Start with 'What are we here for?' and work through vision, ideals and beliefs to goals, targets, changes and projects. Provide the budget outlines as input to the discussion. Identify broadly the constraints and take some decisions. Decisions will be a mixture. Perhaps the agreement and adoption of a mission statement, a change of policy, setting up a working party to investigate an idea and report back at a follow up meeting. As issues get sorted out and progress made, the plan becomes, not some horrendous numbers exercise, but the way that ideas get explored and decisions taken.

Some Techniques

Getting people to break out of the old ways, especially of the ways they see themselves and their potential, is tough. There are some techniques that can help.

ZERO BASE PLAN

Instead of allowing anyone sight of the previous year's figures you ask them to work out what they think they need from scratch. Every item and expense has to be justified in its own right. What usually happens with this approach is that everyone works out the answer from their copy of last year and then spends much time and effort concealing the tracks.

WHAT ARE THE IMPACTS OF MANAGING WITH 10%, 20%, 30%, 40% LESS?

This question gives an amount of money and asks the budget holder to work out how to make it stretch and what will have to be cut out. The seasoned response is to list all the projects dear to the Chairman's heart as facing the chop.

PRIORITISE ACTIVITIES

This method asks budget holders to split their spend up by project and to rank them in order of importance. The least important projects are cut.

WHAT CAN YOU DO WITH MORE MONEY?

This flushes out the ideas that are being held back because someone thinks that they are unaffordable or are nervous of making the suggestion. They may be more worthwhile than some of the things already happening.

None of these approaches will necessarily get a result, but each has its day when asking the question from a slightly different angle and can help unblock thinking.

Making the Plan Work

Once a plan is created it needs to be used. Incorporate the figures into regular reports. Use it as a yardstick to judge new proposals against – does that leave us better off or worse off than the plan assumed? It is a checklist of planned actions. Record progress against it.

The annual accounts are usually read once, not understood, and filed until next year or thrown away. Make the committee keep their copy of the plan to hand to refer to. The more it is used the better will be the understanding of the financial facts by the committee as a whole and the better informed their decisions.

6
MEETINGS AND REPORTING

Role

The Treasurer attends committee and general meetings as a specialist. He has objective financial facts to show, but he should also have a view on what they mean and what, if anything, needs to be done about them. He should spell out the financial issues clearly so that the group themselves can take informed decisions.

Preparation

The first task is to decide how you are going to review the financial position yourself, quite separate from how you later decide to present it to others. You need to look at what has happened, and looks likely to happen, against some kind of framework or background that enables you to make sense of the figures.

Cash Position

The bank reconciliation tells you how much is in the bank after all the cheques made out have been presented. Start from the reconciled balance and set out any invoices that need paying, standing charges, and an estimate of other outgoings for the coming month.

Next, take a view of the income you feel you can depend on. In effect you are estimating how you think the cash book will read in one month's time.

Where will that leave you at the end of next month? Is that a problem? Test the forecast. Are there any likely risks that you have not built in? Invoices that could come in early and need to be paid? Is there a chance that some of your income could be delayed? What impact would one or both of these have?

Your workings will look something like figure 16.

Now that you have wrestled with the estimate yourself you can prepare a simple summary to communicate to the committee (see figure 17).

Cash Book balances 31st March	------------
Less: Expected payments for April	(............)
Expected receipts for April	....
Estimated Cash Book balance end April	------------

Figure 16

Latest cash position	....
Next month cash position	....
Next month low estimate	....

Figure 17

If you keep a record of these figures each month you will give yourself a view of any trends, and also find out how confident you ought to be about your forecasting techniques. Using a PC to plot the figures on a graph or bar chart can be illuminating but a sheet of A4 will do the basics (figure 18).

Cash Forecast History

	Actual	F'cast	Low side	Notes
Opening	1500			
January		1200	900	
February				
March				

Figure 18

This is the first forecast. Next month you fill in the actual for the end of January and the forecasts for February. It should not take long each month to scan through and work out roughly why the actual cash book balance was different from forecast. If you note down the reasons for the variance each time, you will gradually develop an awareness of the things likely to throw out the estimates. It also helps you to pick up problems early. Reporting the cash position and cash forecast answers the most common question committee members ask: 'How much have we got in the bank?' It also answers the one they would like to ask: 'Is there a cash problem?'

Period To Date Receipts and Payments

If you are using a manual cash book, the period to date totals will be the easiest to extract. They also give you a very large part of the story for little effort. With a PC the scope for calculating and presenting all sorts of detail is endless: monthly movements, monthly movement compared to budget, this month compared to this month last year, this month compared to last month.

Before you look at any of these, consider whether the figures are big enough to have any statistical significance. You want to understand the reality described or concealed by the figures and to interpret it to your colleagues, with the least effort possible. If the year, or period to date figures, give you a picture that you can understand and communicate, they are probably adequate for your purpose. At least use them as a start point from which you can decide whether or not you need to go deeper.

Year to date abbreviates to 'YTD'. You can prepare a standard work sheet with all the headings so that you can fill them in by hand from the cash book. Receipts less payments equals the raw surplus or deficit for the year so far. It should tie up with the movement on your cash page.

Last Year

If you do not use a plan, putting last year's actual performance on the page gives some rough yardstick to judge this year against. You do need to be clear in your own mind as to what kind of a measure it is. If last year was a disaster it will be no comfort to be in line with it (figure 19).

August	Actual Year to Date	Last Year
Total receipts	5376	8500

Figure 19

The basic chart can be prepared at the start of the year. Take 11 copies and fill in the year to date figure each month.

Plan

Putting the full year plan figures on the chart starts to give you a feel for where you are going compared to where you are trying to go (figure 20).

August	Actual Year to Date	Plan	Last Year
Total receipts	5376	9000	8500

Figure 20

You are still able to produce the chart at the beginning of the year and take 11 copies.

Percentage Achievement

Compare results with where you would expect to be if each month were roughly 8–9% of the total. If you were on around 25% of plan at the end of March and 50% at the end of June your performance would be fairly smooth and might indicate that you were comfortably close to plan. Calculating the percentage achievement shows you the arithmetical relationship without too much effort. Is £5376 ahead, behind or about right? (See figure 21.)

August (67%)	Actual Year to Date	Plan	Last Year	% Ach
Total receipts	5376	9000	8500	60%

Figure 21

Using the percentage shows us that the achievement is behind a 'straight line'. Is this a problem or not?

Research the Problem

Once you have looked at the overall figures, check the facts. Refer back to the detailed plan schedule and note on it how things are going against what you thought was going to happen. What has changed? What happened that you did not expect? What was better or worse? What did not take place that you thought would? If the shortfall between the August position and straight line is because a couple of fund-raisers were re-scheduled for later in the year there may be no problem.

Decide what this information means to the complete picture? What needs to be done?

WHAT IS REQUIRED TO ACHIEVE THE PLAN?

If there is a problem, try to work out how big it is and look at other lines where you may be able to save money to pay for it. However, if you have issued budgets and agreed that they are reasonable, you will not make friends by trying to cut them unilaterally. Worse, if you keep your ideas about how the savings can be achieved to yourself, and rely on a hunch that everything will work out, do not be surprised when the bills arrive wiping out the imagined savings.

Presenting the Picture

It is tempting, especially when you have spent time and effort looking at the problems and the figures, to try to bring everyone else up to the same thorough understanding of the financial position that you have yourself. You owe it to the committee not to do it. The other trap is to assume that everyone else is as familiar with the figures as you are. A way of giving people the facts but concentrating discussion on the areas you are worried about is a standard form where you actually say what you think. The design is down to you. It could be the same sheet you use to analyse the figures in detail. It could be mostly words.

See figure 22. This is your menu. The comment column can be a tick – 'under control'; or a cross – 'needs sorting out'. If the income side is in shape you need not waste time saying so – they can see that from the chart. If there is an element that you want to draw particular attention to this month, use the spaces below the totals.

If the chart is all ticks and there are no problems, say so and get off. If you want to provide more information, add supplementary charts but please do not ask everyone to turn over while you read aloud what they say. Concentrate on the issues.

Financial Summary

	Actual YTD	Full Year Plan	Comment
Total receipts	£	£	
....			
....			
Total payments	£	£	
....			
....			
Cash position	£	£	
Items from last meeting			
New items			
Matters of report			
Overall rating			

Figure 22 Suggested layout for a financial summary

It is fair to provide an update on the things discussed at the last meeting. Again the tick and cross system saves time. Apart from saying thank you the point is to get agreement on the things that are still problems, not to go over the ones that have been solved.

Matters of report are not only problem related. You may record the results of fund-raising efforts, purchase of equipment, successful re-negotiation of a lease, receipt of a grant or completion of a project. They can be where you appreciate others' efforts. They are brief summaries of things you want people to know about.

Handling Problems

The summary should prompt discussion of the problems you have highlighted. A standard form can be useful here too (see figure 23).

Problem	Duplicator unreliable
Date	March (year)
Description	The last copy of the newsletter could not be duplicated. The maintenance engineer says he cannot get the necessary parts.
Estimated impact	£ various
Options Considered	New duplicator Another second hand duplicator Photocopier New generation copy-printer
Timescale	Needs resolving by June
Recommendation	Full study of costs and technical aspects.
Decision taken	Working group formed. Report back April.

Figure 23 Problem summary sheet

When you have drafted the problem sheet give it to someone else to read and ask them to explain back to you how they see it. If you find yourself arguing that they have misunderstood the point, try again. Write in plain English. It is not supposed to be a MENSA test. Use the figures to tell the story, not to baffle. If you cannot put it over simply maybe you do not understand it yourself yet.

Using a standard format helps the secretary. A copy can be

kept with the minutes. Try to provide copies of both the standard report and the issue sheet to the other committee members before you discuss them, preferably before the meeting.

Recording Decisions

This is usually the most contentious item. Everyone leaves in complete agreement; next month you find that they all agreed something completely different. If you have the use of an overhead projector a good discipline is to write up the agreed actions, with the initials of whoever is responsible for carrying them out alongside. At the end the secretary runs through and secures approval that they are correct. If there is no overhead projector the secretary can still read out actions and responsibilities before the meeting breaks up.

Follow Up

If it was worth raising, it is worth keeping track of. Keep bringing items up until you are happy.

Adding Value

Your standard report provides the basic information on cash position and progress to date. It calls out problems in time to do something about them. There is more you can do to build up the knowledge available to the committee to base decisions on. Consider what projects you can keep a record of and what information would be useful for them to see. Keep detailed debriefing notes on fund-raising events or other activities in a file for future reference. Keep business case summaries and annotate them to show how things actually turned out. Gradually you will build up a valuable set of data which others can go to for background, and which you, and your successors, can use in future evaluations.

7
FINANCIAL TECHNIQUES

Introduction

When the Chairman comes up with another great idea, how do you evaluate it financially? There is no single approach to working out the best choice, or the best financial choice, that can be used every time. There are a number of ways of looking at the problem – a range of 'financial techniques'.

Deciding what 'cost' is can be a nightmare. Common sense says that cost is very straightforward. Sometimes it is. Often the knack is to look at the different ideas of cost and then to decide which ones give the most useful insight on this decision. Forecasts and estimates are more or less scientific terms for guesses. How do you assess the guess? You need to look at a wide spread of what could happen and find where the risks are. Ask yourself what can go wrong?

Working through these approaches to a proposal will give you a different angle of view from the one presented to you for decision. You then need to communicate that new angle to the rest of the committee or membership, explaining the ideas used and convincing them. This involves a bit of magic, sometimes known as a 'business case'.

What Will it Cost?

CAPITAL COST AND RUNNING COST

A group of head teachers were looking at the costs of installing a swimming pool for one of their schools. It was part of a seminar on financial techniques. We were looking at their real life projects. The costs of building and installing the pool were to hand. A small covered pool, capable of being used three seasons out of four, would cost £30,000. Everyone felt that this project would have no problem in attracting the right kind of enthusiastic parental support to raise the cash needed to build it. Teaching children to swim at junior school age was unanimously supported. A super project, but there was a very clear split in views. The heads who had pools would gladly have given them up. Those who did not have them were all enthusiastic about the idea of building. Why the difference?

So we looked at the costs of running it.

Heating £500 for a ten week summer season, how much more for 30 or 40 weeks?

Chemicals and maintenance £1000 per year

Cover and vandalism repairs £300 per year minimum (plus the appeal to parents to mount patrols in the evenings)

ASA qualified instructors £10 per hour

Teacher and administration time? Insurance cover? Regulations over surveillance and supervision?

The picture developed of a facility which absorbed a lot of time, money and management effort to run it safely. Most of the schools ran their pools only for a few weeks in the summer term. It was the only way that they could afford the operating cost within their budgets.

The first discussions concentrated on the building cost, on pros and cons of different designs – raised, sunk, types of cover etc. These were easy to grasp and visualise, therefore to be enthusiastic about. Looking at the cost of running the beast was a dampener.

The swimming pool example is just one. The principle applies equally to minibuses, heating systems, additional buildings. Consider the running costs before you begin, not as an afterthought.

EXPECTED LIFE

The church organ is knackered. The choice seems to narrow down to one of three:

recondition of the current organ	£25,000
replacement with new pipe organ	£125,000
replacement with electronic organ	£40,000

What is the best value for money? The organ was substantially reconditioned about 40 years ago. Here we are again with the problem. One view sees the lives as

recondition	5 years	£5,000 per year
new pipe	50 years	£2,500 per year
electronic	10 years	£4,000 per year

On that basis the new pipe organ gives the cheapest annual cost, even though it is far and away the biggest total outlay. Total cost divided by expected life is a useful measure. Cost per year, cost per month are ideas easily grasped, and usually trotted out to try to sell you an expensive option. Picking the life for each option could be a means of influencing your decision, part of the sales pitch. How confident are you that the estimates look reasonable? Can you back them up with experience? How does the picture change if you use different projected lives? What is a reasonable spread or range? Use a range of lives for each option, as in figure 24.

Option	Total Cost	Shortest		Expected		Longest	
		Yrs	CPY*	Yrs	CPY*	Yrs	CPY*
Recondition	£25000	5	£5000	20	£1250	40	£625
New pipe	£125000	25	£5000	50	£2500	75	£1666
Electronic	£40000	5	£8000	10	£4000	20	£2000

* (cost per year)

Figure 24

There are lies, damned lies, statistics and angled financial evaluations. Test the assumptions.

OPPORTUNITY COST

If someone is pushing for a Yes/No decision, try asking, 'If I do this what else will I not be able to do as a result?' Look not just at the project itself, but at what it stops you doing. One area where this approach works is on using scarce resources – money is generally scarce, but time and enthusiasm can be also. In the first case of the swimming pool it would be appropriate to ask what other uses could be made of £30,000, either if it is available or if it can be raised. All projects will be worthwhile. How do they compare? What are the priorities? What are the benefits?

For one side of opportunity cost – what do I have to give up if I do this? – take an example of a decision over where to hold a jumble sale. The facts look like:

	Our hall	Rented hall
Rental cost	nil	£50
Usual jumble take	£150	£200
Profit	£150	£150

Figure 25

The background to this case is that the rental hall is in an area where jumble sales average more. Where does opportunity cost come in? You find that, in order to use your own hall, you have to turn down two £40 bookings. There is an £80 'opportunity cost', even though it will not show up in the accounts. The rented hall now looks a more profitable bet.

Looking at the cost of not doing something else is a powerful concept. The idea goes beyond the purely financial. Which fund-raising projects should be chosen to get the most money for the least effort? If a big event exhausts the whole membership for the year for £1000, what is the opportunity cost in terms of other ideas that cannot be run?

ALL SORTS OF COSTS

Back to our head teachers and the swimming pool. A commercial organisation wants to use the school pool for a week in the holidays. What does it cost you? Which costs should you consider?

a) marginal cost – the extra costs of using the pool for one more week: heating, chemicals, cleaning, caretaker time. If the caretaker was on duty anyway this would possibly net down to heating and chemicals. The focus here is on the additional cost of doing something.

b) variable cost – the costs that will change as a result of additional use. This can be almost identical with marginal cost. It is usually considered alongside 'fixed' cost – the costs that are there no matter what the level of use. In this case the 'fixed' costs of the pool might only be the insurance.

c) full cost – this would include all the costs which showed against the swimming pool, but might also go beyond it to take a share of the basic administrative cost of running the school. It would also include some figure for 'wear and tear' or the original cost of building and installation.

d) contribution – if the marginal (or variable) costs of using the pool are £20 per day, and the company offers £40 per day, you have a £20 per day contribution towards your fixed costs. When you take all the fixed costs involved into consideration you may find that the pool actually has a 'full cost' of £50 per day. Contribution is not the same thing as profit. What contribution tells you is how much better off you will be as a result of a one-off decision. It is what you have left over after covering the 'marginal' costs. Which cost do you use for which decision?

	One off use	Regular use
Offer below marginal cost	REJECT	REJECT
Offer equals marginal cost	?	REJECT
Offer more than marginal cost but below full cost	ACCEPT	?
Offer at full cost or better	ACCEPT	ACCEPT

There is a rule of thumb. If it is a one-off, bite their arm off for any cash over marginal cost. If the project is going to be repeated regularly, make sure that you understand all the impacts before you commit to it.

Trying to understand your costs in terms of fixed and variable will be valuable even with a rough exercise. The broader use of this information is to examine rates used for regular lettings. A church was used by another group for weekly worship. They made a donation of a few hundred pounds per year. When examined, the donation only just covered heat and light. It made no contribution to the longer term costs of building upkeep and cleaning. A discussion of the 'full costs' of making the church available resulted in a more generous donation.

Price Decisions

Having worked through a long exercise on costs, for example the church hall, how do you use this information to set prices? With care. Prices do not need to have any relation to cost unless you want them to. If you have a policy of charging nominal rates to other charities, then by all means analyse and use the costs to decide how much to charge the Brownies. Charging for a wedding party is another matter. What can you charge and still keep the business? How do your rates compare with other facilities in the area? Marginal costs set the lowest level you can accept without losing money. The only upper limit is what people will pay. Understand your costs, but look to the market to set your prices. Getting the highest possible rates for use of the hall may be the single most important contribution you can make – worth hundreds of hours of fund-raising.

CONSTRAINTS

What things set limits to what you can choose? Available space, fire regulations, bye-laws governing noise, the number of volunteers, the time available, existing use of premises? Note what you believe the main constraints to be and think about how this might affect the price you set and the style of the offering. At a silent auction, with a capacity limit of 120, the decision was to offer unlimited food and drink for a high, all inclusive price. Why? Given that 120 people was the maximum, pushing the price up meant that the people who came were well enough off to spend a decent amount at the auction.

PERCEIVED VALUE

Turn the idea round. Why would anyone in their right mind want this at this price? The answer can be baffling – how many people actually like coconuts? Yet they pay good money to win them.

Value for money is evasive, tied in to the oddities of human nature and taste, but you should at least consider it. Whatever you are 'selling' – tickets to a concert, tombola, entrance to a jumble sale – try to look at it from the punter's point of view. Which emotional pocket will the money come from? Entertainment, gambling or good works? What will affect a decision to attend or not attend, to buy or not to buy?

Once you have thought through this perspective, go back to the price decision and sketch out your evaluation, as has been done for a barn dance for the local school in figure 26.

Constraint

Hall capacity		120 people
(including tables & room to dance)		

Costs

Fixed	Hire of band	£200
Variable	Ploughman's @ £1 per head	
Drink	Sale or return	

Price

Standard pricing in the area is £2–3 without food and £4–5 with food. There seems to be a psychological barrier at the £5 mark.

Evaluation of ticket price

	£2	£3	£4	£5
Ticket sales 120 people	£240	£360	£480	£600
Band	(£200)	(£200)	(£200)	(£200)
Food @ £1 per head	—	—	(£120)	(£120)
Tickets, posters, etc.	(£40)	(£40)	(£40)	(£40)
Profit	—	£120	£120	£240

Figure 26 Summary to evaluate ticket prices

OTHER VALUES

What do you want from the event? The financial evaluation is laid out, but it is not the whole picture. The choice has to take into account all sorts of other factors. Will a £5 ticket price tip the scale too far for some members who you would really like to be there? Is the objective mainly fund-raising or social? Are you building a reputation for value for money or ripping them off? Note though, how the financial choices can help to thrash out the other values.

Forecasts

In business a forecast is often the lowest figure that will make the project look attractive enough to get approval. Forecasting is tied in with risk – the risk of getting it wrong – as much as it is about making accurate estimates of the future. Concentrate on the risk aspect.

BREAKEVEN

Irrespective of what anyone says is likely to happen, what is the worst result that will cover the costs? Do you believe that this at least is safe? A prestigious choral society offers to give a concert in aid of the organ appeal. Their services would be free but a semi-professional orchestra would need to be hired, soloists paid and out of pocket expenses covered. They recommend a ticket price of £4. The church holds about 400 people comfortably (if a wooden pew can ever be described as comfortable).

Cost estimates are:

Orchestra	£200
Soloists	£400
Chorus expenses	£150
Advertising	£ 50
Total Marginal cost	£800

The breakeven is the worst result that will at least cover costs. At £4 per ticket we would need to sell 200 tickets to get to break even (200 × £4 = £800). Experience tells us that the worst turn out should be 100. The best could only be 400. This gives a range of possibilities (see figure 27).

The decision still needs to be explored and tested. How confident is the committee that the event will be attractive? How many tickets do individual members believe that they can sell? How many regular followers of this choral society will turn

	Worst	Breakeven	Predicted	Best
Tickets sold	100	200	300	400
Sales @ £4	£400	£800	£1200	£1600
Costs	(£800)	(£800)	(£800)	(£800)
Profit/(loss)	(£400)	—	£400	£800

Figure 27 Breakeven analysis

out in addition to our own locals? What happened the last time a similar event was held?

Breakeven is a good quick test of whether an idea has a reasonable chance of success. If breakeven looks difficult, use it to drive for actions to bring the risk down. How this one is solved is down to the ingenuity of the organising team. They could run another event beforehand, appeal for sponsorship, negotiate a sharing of costs, commit to sell a given number of tickets or agree to underwrite the risk personally. Avoid being negative. 'There's no way this will make money' becomes, 'What can be done to reduce the risk?'

PLUCKING FIGURES FROM THE AIR

'100,000 people live in this town. We only need a one per cent turn out to get a thousand people. I think we can safely go for 5 per cent. 5,000 people, spending £5 each – £25,000. We'll raise a fortune.'

Estimates have to come from somewhere. Try to get them from somewhere reliable. It is generally more useful to look at previous examples of similar things, with a wary eye for key points of difference. Do not project statistics off big meaningless numbers. Estimate what you need to know to take the decision.

For a school raffle the statistics were as shown in figure 28.

The decision to go ahead did not need a forecast of what would happen, just a judgement that a minimum level could be beaten. This concentration on making sure things will not lose money may seem negative. It is not. Wherever possible you want to be able to say 'Yes' to new ideas and initiatives. Directing attention to covering breakeven sets a low, but safe, hurdle. It lets you support new ideas as long as they can cover their costs.

Number of children in school		950
Raffle tickets printed		10000
Price 20p each in books of 5		
Total possible sales		£2000
Cost of prizes	£200	
Cost of printing	£ 75	
Two books were to be given to each child		

	25% take up	50% take up	75% take up
Books of tickets sold (at £1 each)	£475	£950	£1425
Costs	(£275)	(£275)	(£275)
Profit	£200	£675	£1150

Figure 28 Statistics for establishing feasibility of running a raffle

SENSITIVITY ANALYSIS

The choral concert mentioned earlier only really had one thing which could vary – the number of tickets sold. Most events or projects have a number of different things which can go either way – for you or against you.

Our head teachers also looked at a nursery project. There was a capital cost of £20,000. Project life was thought to be around 20 years. As it was a commercial idea a bank loan would be used. See figure 29.

Income calculation N children at £N per week/term

Cost profile
Staff salaries: £8,000 per qualified worker year
Cleaning
Heat & light
Insurance
Financing costs: £20,000 at N%

Variables
number of children
price per child
wages cost
general inflation
cost of borrowing

Figure 29 Elements used in testing the nursery project

By calculating the effect of changing each element you can identify where the risk lies, as shown in figure 30.

Cost of borrowing	
Cost of borrowing today 10%	£2000 per year
Cost of additional 1% on interest rate	£200 per year
Cost at 15%	£3000 per year
Impact of 15% interest rate	£1000 negative p/y
Cost of qualified staff	
Cost today per 'man year'	£8000
Number of 'man years' needed	3
Annual cost for 3 'man years'	£24000
Effect of 5% wage increase	£1200 per year
Effect of 10% wage increase	£2400 per year
Effect of additional person	£8000

Figure 30 Analysing the 'risks'

Each 'risk' was reviewed to see the impact it would have on the profitability of the project. The proposal had looked easy to understand, because the judgements were silently built into it. Figures had been selected for numbers of children and a target price. By insisting that each item could and would move, and trying to guess by how much, the proposal was tested and the weak points discovered.

The Business Case

A little magic helps. Once the committee gets used to the idea of bashing a project around to test out the angles they can get enthusiastic about the process. Before long, no matter who has the bright idea, someone else will pipe up with, 'But what does the business case look like?' Working through a business case invites others to join in. If you use the approach that there are no eternal rules, that the best estimates are only educated guesswork, and that you are looking for as wide a view as possible, then everyone can contribute, and will.

Using ranges, rather than a single set of figures, makes them less contentious. 'Do we believe the answer is somewhere between?' is easier to work with than 'this is the forecast'. Identifying the risks (mostly you are concerned with avoiding disaster) can stimulate proposals of action to eliminate them.

The 'business case', or whatever else you choose to call it, gives everyone a structure to discuss and debate, and a formal way of recording decisions.

Putting the Techniques to Work

Business case for Summer Fête.

ASSESS TRACK RECORD

Who is the co-ordinator for the project? What have they achieved before? Is this a regular event that operates like clockwork or a new venture into untested territory? Do we know what we are doing? Does the scale of the event match our known skills and resources?

This is not a charter for discouraging new ideas. It is possible to break totally new ground and run a huge unprecedented event successfully, like Live Aid back in 1985. It just needs closer care to ensure that the team know what they are up to. Live Aid may have been unprecedented as a Charity event, but the people involved knew all the angles of running similar business events. The expertise was sound. You want to know why the event will be a success.

ANALYSE THE RISKS

They tend to net down to 'nobody comes'.

Summer Fêtes — Rain
F.A. Cup Final
County reach cricket one day final
5 other fêtes same day

Christmas Bazaars — Rain and snow
New super-store opens across town
Football/rugby

Concert — Advance ticket sales fail
Band goes down with flu on night
Heating breaks down

Look at the most likely problems. How likely is likely? Find ways of beating them, or at least bear them in mind as you plan.

DOCUMENT THE COSTS

Hire of site/facility
Hire of equipment
Expenses and fees for 'attractions' and professionals
Advertising
Insurance

Printing
Cost of products and prizes for re-sale

The organiser should be able to draw up a rough budget outline. How much are the 'up-front' costs? What is the amount at risk if the whole event gets washed out?

PROJECT THE RETURN

What were last year's gross takings? What will be different this year? If a new project, what does the organiser think he can achieve? Why? The local papers will contain data every week about how much similar events have raised, but be wary. Is it gross or net? Does it include the proceeds of a grand draw? Was it sponsored? The figures quoted will tend to be the most optimistic view.

CONSTRUCT THE WHOLE PICTURE

Summer Fête: Business Case Evaluation

Organising team	Unchanged from last year		
Risks	Rain		
Costs	Insurance	£100	
	Public address system	£125	
	Attractions	£220	
	Advertising & printing	£100	
	Up front		£545
	Food, drink & prizes		£300
	Total costs		£845
Return	Last year grossed £1500		
	Additional sideshows, bigger tombola & barbecue		
	Organiser's estimate	£1750–£2000	
Key issues	Weather – need 'if wet' plan (insurance cost vs benefit)		
	Competition/clashing events		
	Effectiveness of advertising		
Range of outcomes	Worst: lose up-front costs of £545		
	Best: £2000 less £845 costs = £1155		

Figure 31

WHAT CAN YOU CHANGE?

You are still at the planning stage, with a draft business case to discuss with the committee. The whole point of the exercise is improvement. Explore ways of changing this picture. This is a fund-raiser, how can you make it raise more and cost less? Challenge every item in the list of expenses as to why it is there and why at that cost. The following are all concrete examples from recent years:

Insurance – our existing policy covered us for activities run on our property. By squeezing the scale down we got a cosy, slightly cramped fête with no additional premiums.

Public address system – avoided by borrowing a basic system and scrounging a couple of outside speakers. Only achieved by having someone with the right expertise on the team.

Attractions – arena events replaced by 'It's A Knockout' type competition. Virtually free and guaranteed a good turn out just from the number of competitors. Other attractions were offered a pitch to run a stall for their own account, for a fee. This needs care and attention though. At one village fête an outsider offered to lay on a beer tent free of charge. He would give a donation from his profits. It was a boiling hot afternoon, the beer tent was packed, and the donation was small.

Advertising & printing – turned from expense into profit by sale of advertising and advance sales of the programme.

Food – sale or return plus concentration on high quality products that organisers were committed to buy if not used. Alternative strategy was to buy minimum requirement and have flying squad ready to purchase additional as and when needed.

Some of these ideas come across as penny pinching. It is possible to get into unproductive fights with the organising team – phrases like 'spoiling the ship for a ha'porth of tar' are not unknown. I prefer to ask the question. 'How can we get to the morning of the event and be in profit before it begins?' Faced with this particular outline, and the fact that last year's fête had been washed out, actions taken were:

1) quiz night held to underwrite up front costs
2) donations obtained to put a grand draw together
3) advertising sold to cover cost of programme and show a profit.

PUBLISH THE OUTLINE PLAN

Once the outline 'business case', and the improvement actions are agreed, get the committee to approve it and publish it. Make clear what level of variance is acceptable without reference to you. If the outline plan shows up-front costs of £500, does that mean £500 to £550, no more than £500 or tell me if it goes past £600? Make sure that you and the organiser understand each other.

AFTERWARDS

As soon as you can, publish the results in as close a shape to the business case as is possible. De-brief on success and failure and set out ideas for next time, including whether there will be one.

Conclusion on Financial Techniques

Looking at costs, identifying risk, testing forecasts; the common ingredients to all this are the willingness to ask hard questions and to take more than one view of the problem. All you need are common sense, arithmetic and a nose for disaster.

8
TIPS ON FINANCE FOR SMALL SCALE EVENTS

Floats

Make them up well beforehand. Not having floats ready to hand out in good time is a lynching offence as far as the other helpers are concerned. Get the organiser to tell you which stalls there will be and make up two more than that. Keep a central reserve float to deal with the £20 notes that turn up in the first five minutes.

I keep a stock of large, stackable, margarine tubs to issue them in.

Tickets

Pre-number them. Keep a list of those to whom the tickets have been distributed. Follow it through to tickets returned and cash received.

Monitor how efficient your controls really are. If half the people with tickets tell you at the door that they have not paid, the system did not work. You can try using a box on the ticket for your sellers to mark 'NOT PAID'. Alternatively, make it clear that you will collect all money at the door. Try to find a system that works for your organisation and get people used to it.

Jumble Sales & Bazaars

SPOTTING THE VALUABLES

Debates rage over whether helpers should get first pick or not. Get someone knowledgeable to go through the jumble looking for valuable items. Sell them through the antiques trade or at auction.

THE DOOR

People will try to:

a) get in before the sale start time
b) get in free.

This is war.

1. Put two helpers, not one, preferably large, on the door. Use tables and chairs to slow the traffic and make the entrance narrow.
2. Accept donated goods in an outer lobby and have them transferred by accredited helpers into the hall. This avoids the 'helper' who turns up with a black sack of utterly valueless junk who just has to come through to deliver it.
3. Brief everyone on the arrangements beforehand.
4. Watch out for:
   'I'm helping'
   'I'm with . . . They've already paid for me.'
   'I paid the last time.'
   'I've only been out for a breath of fresh air/to the toilet.'
   The large group who slap down a pile of coppers and bulldoze through.

SECURITY INSIDE

Have more helpers rather than less. Provide reliefs. Have a couple or more floating supervisors visibly active as a deterrent against theft. Keep cash tubs out of reach.

COUNTING

Counting during the event can help to raise morale – you can let everyone know the latest figure and spur them on to greater things. You should also be able to declare a result within half an hour of the end. It is a team effort.

You need:

a) a safe space with a large table
b) plastic bags from the bank
c) an analysis sheet with all stalls listed
d) a cash counting tray for loose change – borrow one from the bank.

Set out on the analysis sheet each of the stalls in action, or table numbers.

The format could be as shown in figure 32.

After the first half hour or hour, send the collecting team out to retrieve surplus cash. A card can be kept in each tub which is annotated for the amount taken. Better still, use a small duplicate receipt book and put the top copy in the tub. Agree the amount taken with the stall holder – it tells them how they are doing.

Stall		Float issued	Count 1	Count 2	Count 3	Final Gross	Float repaid	Net takings
Toys	£	(10)	15.00	10.00	3.67	28.67	(10)	18.67
Crafts	£	(10)	55.00	30.00	14.23	99.23	(10)	89.23
xxxx	£							
Totals								

Figure 32 Analysis sheet for stalls

Re-count the total cash at the control centre and note any discrepancies at the foot of the column. Communicate the 'cash so far' figure to the helpers.

Repeat the process at intervals. Take the larger denominations first: notes, £1 coins, 50p coins. Bag them up as you go, using the plastic bags provided on request by all the high street banks.

At the end, ask each stall to count their remaining cash and bring it in. This should not be more than a few pounds.

Using the sheet, you can declare a provisional total, subject to count, straightaway. When you prepare the paying in sheet for the bank there will probably be a small difference. Show it on the control sheet as 'counting difference'. Get the counting team to countersign against their names, and declare the final result. Because the bulk of the money has been counted and bagged up before the end, it really is possible to publish the final result before the clearing up is finished.

Security Afterwards

Check the insurance position. Up to what value is loose cash in the safe covered? Which officials are insured to hold cash? If your bank operate a night safe facility, even if only for notes, this is preferable to taking it home.

Designing Procedures

It is always worth sitting down with the organisers to work out how you are going to handle the cash, especially for a new idea. Analyse what will happen and how to deal with it.

This example is for a 'Silent Auction'.

The setting is a hall with a number of tables. Each table has several numbered lots, over 100 in all. People bid for the lots by writing their bid on a lot card, together with their name. The last, and highest bid written at the close secures the article.

Problems:

a) The money is taken, not evenly during the course of the event, but right at the end. You want to collect cash in a controlled way, but quickly.
b) Security of the articles at the end. You do not want to take someone's money, only to find that the item has walked.
c) At some of these auctions it can take ages to pay. Long queues make for disgruntled people, and you want to get home too.

The first decision taken was to pull raffles forward before the close. Otherwise the administration for these would get in the way. The second was to appoint a 'steward' for each table to be responsible for security of items, and handing them over to successful bidders. Thirdly, this is essentially a queuing problem – just like Friday night at the supermarket. You have to have enough 'channels' open to handle the queues.

Process:

At the close of the auction the lot cards are brought to the control table and the winning bids read out. At the cash desk one person writes down name and amount against each lot number. This creates a master record of the bids. Next to him sits a second assistant with a red pen. His job is to confirm the amounts and name against each lot number and tick off the master schedule as each one is paid. In front of him are two or three pairs of cash men, each armed with a 'paid' stamp, a large float, a calculator and a copy of the programme that already has each lot listed and described.

As the name and value are recorded the bidders collect their lot cards. They have the choice of either paying for each one separately or holding on to settle all their purchases in one go.

As soon as the first card is handed back the bidders can settle up at one of the cash points. The card is presented. One of the pair confirms the amount with the controller with the red pen, who ticks off the master schedule. If he uses his red pen deftly, this does not interrupt the other person, who is still writing the master schedule up, but is now further down the page. The second cash point helper handles the cash, gives change, and stamps the card 'paid'.

With the 'paid' lot card as evidence the goods can be collected from the tables, on presentation to the stewards, and removed from the hall.

Comment:

This procedure works. The last payment was collected only minutes after the last bid was read out. A bonus of the big finance team was that we had the cash counted and ready to be paid into the bank within half an hour of the close.

It was not a one man effort. It involved all the organising team. We discussed areas of dissatisfaction with other voluntary and commercial events, and how to avoid them. We ran a trial of the procedure by closing some 'quick lots' at the half way stage. That showed us the need for pairs of helpers at the cash points, keeping recording and cash handling completely separate. Using one person to do both was not fast enough. Bidders did not wait quietly, they barged in and demanded attention.

This example embodies the view I have of the Treasurer's role. Too often it is seen as a backroom job of mind-numbing tedium, incomprehensible to all but qualified accountants. My vision is of someone who handles and provides information, seeking always to involve the whole team in considering and taking decisions. He uses his knowledge and expertise as a way of throwing light on problems and looking for workable solutions, not as a power base or to keep people in the dark. By making finance something that everyone can contribute to, everyone recognises ownership and responsibility for it.

Less sententiously perhaps, the axioms are:

Always keep your eyes open for good ideas and duff ones.
Steal the best.
Test them to make sure they work.
Aim to improve them next time.

9
RECEIPTS AND PAYMENTS ACCOUNTS

Introduction

The preparation of a set of accounts, as against keeping the cash book, is a daunting affair. It involves thinking about the right way to show things. It enters the baffling world of accounting standards. Depending on the legal requirements, eg for a registered charity, there may be a need for expert or professional assistance to ensure that your accounts satisfy those requirements and conform to appropriate standards. But, and it is a big but, they are *your* accounts. You have to be happy that the picture they present is 'true and fair', that the accounts show what happened financially and where you are at the end of the period.

Receipts and Payments Account

Whatever format you use in the end, preparing a receipts and payments account is a first step. It is a straightforward way of presenting the basic accounts. Rule off the cash book, check the additions, prepare a closing bank reconciliation, and then list out the totals for each heading. What you then have is a receipts and payments account.

If you only have one bank account, a small number of transactions in the year, and no assets other than cash, this may be all you need. It is factual and concise. It concentrates on cash. Providing you remember about the bills that need paying it should be quite hard to get anything but a fair picture of the events of the year and how much cash there is at the year end.

The traditional lay-out for a receipts and payments account is shown in figure 33.

Weaknesses with this layout are:

a) It does not show the amount of total payments or total receipts.
b) The reader has to do some mental arithmetic to work out

Najafabad Mothers Group
Receipts and Payments Account (year)

Receipts		**Payments**	
Balance b/fwd			
1 January	£ 80.66		
Subscriptions	99.70	Stationery	£ 2.00
Ploughman's lunch	13.55	Postage	12.41
Bazaar stall net	20.72	Lunches	4.50
Bring & Buy sales	6.85	Cards	3.91
Jumble sales	157.26	Telephone	3.00
Boot sale	50.75	Adverts	5.40
		Other	4.26
		Donations	250.00
		Balance c/fwd	
		31 December	144.01
	£429.49		£429.49

Figure 33 Traditional layout for receipts and payments account

that receipts were bigger than payments and by how much.

c) Two pieces of accounting jargon – 'brought forward' and 'carried forward' add unnecessary doubt as to what is going on.

Another format for the same receipts and payments account could be that shown in figure 34.

With this lay-out the arithmetic is more obvious and easier to follow. The mysteries of 'brought forward' and 'carried forward' have been removed.

The Deposit Account Within Receipts and Payments

If there is a deposit account, and transfers are made backwards and forwards through the year, you can list out two receipts and payments accounts, one for current and one for deposit. The problem is that the movements between the two accounts can obscure the picture. The more frequent the transfers, the bigger the figure becomes, taking the focus off the receipts from, and payments to, outside sources.

Also, instead of a single figure which sums up the change

Najafabad Mothers Group
Receipts and Payments Account (year)

Receipts		
Subscriptions	£ 99.70	
Ploughman's lunch	13.55	
Bazaar stall net	20.72	
Bring & Buy sales	6.85	
Jumble sales	157.26	
Boot sale	50.75	
Total receipts		348.83
Payments		
Stationery	£ 2.00	
Postage	12.41	
Lunches	4.50	
Cards	3.91	
Telephone	3.00	
Adverts	5.40	
Other	4.26	
Donations	250.00	
Less total payments		285.48
Excess of receipts over payments for the year		63.35
Add: balance at 1 January		80.66
Balance at 31 December		£144.01

Figure 34 Alternative format for receipts and payments account

during the year, whether you call it 'surplus', 'deficit', or 'movement', you now have two. Put money onto deposit from current and it can look as though you are losing money on the current account. Showing the naked receipts and payments obscures the underlying story. Without losing the simplicity of the receipts and payments format you can reduce the confusion.

1. Instead of showing the total payments to deposit and the total transfers from deposit (think of it as moving change between left and right trouser pockets – what is important is how much you have, not how many times you move it),

show a single entry for the net movement between the two accounts. Therefore, if the transfers from deposit add up to £6,500 and transfers to deposit were £7,500, show the net impact: £1000 has been transferred to deposit in the year. Show only the £1000 (use the word 'net' by all means) as a payment in the current account and a receipt in the deposit account.

2. Use the neutral phrase 'change in balance' rather than deficit or surplus, in both cases.
3. Bring the picture together by an additional note. For example, see figure 35.

Summary of changes in cash

	Current account	Deposit account	Total
Balances at 1 January	£500	—	£500
Change in balance for the year	(£300)	£1000	£700
Balances at 31 December	£200	£1000	£1200

Figure 35 Use additional notes for clarity

Suspense Account

If there have been a lot of 'ins and outs', show the detail in a note, setting the receipt alongside the payment that goes with it. Show clearly where money still has to be paid out, or is owed.

Statement of Assets and Liabilities

The receipts and payments account only looks at cash. The only balance shown is that in the bank, or owing to it. The true financial picture may be bigger than that. Even for a small club, meeting in a local hall, there may be equipment which has been acquired over the years and which has a value. There may also be bills outstanding at the end of the year which ought to be noted.

Even if you do not need the formality of a balance sheet, you should provide members with information so that they understand what they own and what they owe. A list of assets, showing what they cost, what they are expected to cost to replace and when that is expected, sets the pure cash held in perspective. A list of bills not yet paid underlines the real cash available to spend. If the apparent healthy position was caused by you holding off payment of a big invoice this should be made very clear.

There is room for judgement, but your aim should be to provide the fullest picture of assets and liabilities so that the amount of cash is clearly set in context. Your statement of accounts needs to show not only what has been done with the money, but also what can be done and needs to be done with it.

10
BEYOND RECEIPTS AND PAYMENTS ACCOUNTS

If you want, or are required, to produce more than a receipts and payments account, you need the structure and approach provided by traditional double entry book keeping. This is introduced in the Appendix (see page 137). This chapter is in two sections: first, the logical steps to produce the figures for the raw accounts; and second, the things to consider for the total presentation.

The accounts are made up of:

The opening balances from the previous year.
The transactions in the cash book.
Transactions outside the cash book

* movements direct into or from a deposit account
* items that have not yet gone through the cash book for expense or income
* adjustments for amounts that have gone through the cash book that do not relate to the year
* accounting for capital items and depreciation
* accounting for changes in value of assets, particularly investments.

The job, therefore, is a mixture of organising the information you already have and reviewing other facts to make sure that you provide a full view of the position at the end of the year and of the performance in the year.

The Opening Balances

Last year's balance sheet is your opening list of balances. The presentation may confuse you a little but it should not be too difficult to list them out in two columns for debits and credits. If you can get hold of a piece of wide analysis paper for this it will make life easier. If not, tape two pieces of A4 together, side by side, or use a couple of spare pages in the cash book. You need as many columns as you can get. This listing of balances is called an 'opening trial balance'. It is a way of recording your start point.

The Cash Book Transactions

Leave some space below the first list of balances (the 'balance sheet' section) and then enter the cash book transaction totals in the next two columns, using the headings from the cash book.

The list of receipts will be in the Cr column. The total value of cash received goes in the Dr column, next to the current account balance brought forward.

The list of payments will be in the Dr column, with the total amount of cash paid going in the Cr column, next to the balance brought forward.

If you now add across the cash at bank – balance brought forward in last year's balance sheet – and total receipts less total payments (the debits are positive and the credits negative), you should end up with the balance already struck in the cash book. If there are no accounting adjustments, adding across the page will give you a new list of balances from which you can prepare the draft accounts.

The Deposit Account

(*or high interest cheque account or any other bank account without a separate cash book*)

You have already entered the deposit transfers from current account and to current account and the opening balance. You still have to enter:

a) interest credited direct to the deposit account
b) monies received and paid in direct to the deposit account
c) expenses paid direct from the deposit account.

You now need to bring these transactions, which have not gone through the cash book, 'into account', by entering the details in a journal.

Journal	Dr	Cr
--	--------	--------

Figure 36

The Journal

It can be in a bound book or punched and filed with your other working papers.

For the deposit entries, think of how you would have recorded the entries if they had come into the current account instead of the deposit account. A receipt would be a debit to cash and a credit on the other side.

For example, assume that the entries on the deposit account which came in direct were:

1. Interest credited 30th June £230
2. Interest credited 31st December £225
3. Proceeds of fund-raising paid in 10th October £575

The journal would read

	Dr	Cr
Dr Deposit account	£1030	
Cr Interest account		£455
Cr Fund-raising		£575
	£1030	£1030

'Interest credited by the bank for the year and proceeds of fund-raising paid in direct.
See deposit account statement and pay-in slip.'

Figure 37 Journal entries

Now enter the journalled transactions onto the working sheet in the next two columns. Add across all the entries on the deposit account line and you should now arrive at the balance on the closing bank statement.

If you do not agree the balance, check to make sure you have not missed any transactions and that you have added across correctly, i.e. debits are positive, credits negative.

The movements between current and deposit have now been eliminated. They are neither income nor expenditure and would just inflate the totals on both sides. Apart from the inter-account movements any income or expense in the deposit account is now added on to the normal income or expense line. As a sense check, look at the sheet so far. You have the balances from last year, a list of receipts and payments, and the current and deposit accounts, which, added across, show the year-end balances you recognise.

The Suspense Account

All year you have entered peculiar things into the suspense account, and kept track of what is in there. Now it is time to net the items down and sort out what they mean. If you have not kept a control log you will need to create one. Take a sheet of paper and write down all the receipts on the left and payments on the right. Check that the items add up to the totals in the cash book. Work through, numbering each item and matching off with corresponding entries on the other side. When you have matched off all you can you should be left with a much smaller number of unmatched items. Test your analysis. Add across the suspense account, debits less credits, on your trial balance schedule. Does that balance equal the net figure which your analysis adds up to?

Now consider what they are. When you are happy that you understand each one, transfer it to an appropriate account – money owed to 'creditors', money owing to 'debtors' etc. The suspense account should now be at nil.

Accruals and Pre-payments

Accruals are the adjustments you make to the accounts to show

a) bills not paid which relate to the period
b) estimates of amounts owing for work done or services received which have not been invoiced yet
c) amounts paid for things or services not yet used.

They are required by the 'matching' principle – that the expenditure shown should relate to the income generated, or, in the voluntary case, to the period and the activities. Recognise what you have used rather than only what you have paid for.

One Treasurer I knew hated the idea that her final accounts did not look like her cash book. She disliked making adjustments for 'accruals'. The solution she found was to pay all the outstanding bills by cheque on 31st December and delay paying any bills for services in advance – like insurance – until January 1st. Another method is to get the bills most likely to be a problem – gas, electricity, telephone or insurance – paid on a monthly budget account.

That way the 'payments' are roughly the same as the expenditure. Whenever you provide a 'receipts and payments' position you are also giving a fair idea of income and expenditure, apart from capital items and movements between investments.

The purpose of accruals and pre-payments is to get the financial position as near right as possible. That does not mean right to the nearest penny. A reasonable approximation is fine.

RECOMMENDED CHECKLIST FOR ACCRUALS AND PRE-PAYMENTS REVIEW

Gas
Electricity
Telephone
Repairs not yet invoiced
Contracts in progress
Insurance
Rent
Office supplies invoiced monthly
Heating oil stocks

You ought to have a good idea of what is happening that could result in invoices arriving after the end of the period for work or goods received and used in the period. However, it is worth checking with any other members of the committee who have authority to order work to be done whether there are any other liabilities.

For the utilities – gas, electricity and telephone – the bill is often complicated by standing charges which are paid in advance. Keep the calculations simple, or read the meters to be really precise. For example, see figure 38.

Year end 31 December

Gas bill. Quarter ended 31 October: £300

Simple estimate
November and December to come
Average usage £100 per month
Accrue two months at £100 = £200

Refined estimate
November and December to come
Winter usage £125 per month
Accrue two months at £125 = £250

Figure 38

Either way the accounts will show roughly a full year's gas bills and help users of the accounts to see trends and not to be comparing 10 months' spend one year with 12 the year before. It will also tell them that £200–£250 of cash is needed to pay a creditor.

The same calculation works for services paid for in advance. If the annual insurance premium is paid on July 1st each year, then the cost of insurance that should be in accounts for the calendar year will be half the premium paid this year plus half the premium paid last year. There is 6 months' value not yet received.

Stock

It may be appropriate to take account of things bought which have not been used if they are of substantial value.

For example, a delivery of oil in mid December is probably for next year's heating. By showing the oil stock as an asset you reduce the amount shown as expenditure for the year.

In this case you would dip the tank as near the period end as possible and show the value of oil in the tank as an asset in the balance sheet.

Examples of accounting for accruals, pre-payments and stock. All examples assume period end of 31 December last year.

1. Electricity bill for quarter to end November last year £220. Not paid until January this year. There is a standing charge of £30 payable in advance for December, January and February. The rest is usage.
   Of the £220, the usage of £190 all belongs to last year.
   Of the £30 standing charge £10 belongs to last year and £20 to this year. I would accrue £200 for this invoice and a further £70 for estimated December usage.
   Total accrual £270.

Journal	Dr	Cr
Dr Heat and light	£270	
Cr Sundry creditors		£270

'Accrual for electricity bill not paid and usage not yet invoiced for December average month.'

Figure 39

2. Insurance premium £500 payable 1st January this year. Not paid until January this year. No action required.
3. Insurance premium £500 dated 1st July last year for year in advance. Paid July last year. Half the invoice value relates to this year.

Journal	Dr	Cr
Dr Pre-payments	£250	
Cr Insurance		£250

'Pre-payment of insurance for 6 months to June (this year).'

Figure 40

4. Copier paper delivered 1st December. Invoice £60 paid 15th December. Roughly two thirds of paper still in stock unused at year-end. Either ignore because the value is small, or treat the unused paper as stock.

Journal	Dr	Cr
Dr Stock	£40	
Cr Stationery expense		£40

'Value of stock held at 31 December (last year).
10 reams at £4 per ream.'

Figure 41

Once you have journalled all the accruals, enter them on the working sheet in the adjustments columns. I find it helpful to write the journal number in a circle at the side of each entry.

Last Year's Accruals and Pre-payments

You should have a copy of last year's journals. When you brought in last year's balance sheet it probably included some balances for straightforward accruals and pre-payments made then. Those entries need to be reversed to take them out of the balance sheet and into income or expense.

Example
Brought forward balances from last year.

Accruals	250 Cr	electricity
Pre-payments	200 Dr	insurance
Stock	90 Dr	paper

(See figure 42 for layout of Journal entries.)

Journal	Dr	Cr
Dr Accruals	£250	
Cr Electricity		£250
'reversal of (last year) accrual. (yr) J5.'		
Dr Insurance	£200	
Cr Pre-payments		£200
'reversal of (last year) payment. (yr) J6.'		
Dr Stationery	£90	
Cr Stock		£90
'reversal of (last year) pre-payment. (yr) J7.'		

Figure 42

Think through the effect of the above entries: the accruals balance was a credit balance. The debit for electricity to the accruals reduces that balance and the credit shows like a cash receipt against electricity, it reduces the expense. That part of the electricity bill related to the previous year and was dealt with then.

Other Brought Forward Balances From Last Year
You should have checked these out when you took over. Before you take any accounting action you need to understand what they represent and the facts as they stand today.

Capital and Depreciation

If you capitalise and depreciate you should have two accounts for each asset, or type of asset, that go in the balance sheet:

Cost account (Dr)

Provision for depreciation account (Cr)

There will also be a depreciation expense account which feeds into the Income and Expenditure account.

You should be able to work out from the first two accounts how much the asset cost, when it was bought and how quickly it is being written off. Work out the calculation for the year's depreciation on each asset. You cannot depreciate beyond nil value.

The double entry is shown in figure 43.

Journal	Dr	Cr
Dr Depreciation expense	£xxx	
Cr Provision for depreciation		£xxx

Figure 43 Double entry

If any capital items were bought in the year you need to decide what their useful life is. Often it is possible to come up with some rough approximations – 5 years seems to be a standard choice for office equipment and cars.

Changes in Value of Investments

Until quite recently the ruling commercial principle was that investments should be shown in the balance sheet at the lower of cost or market price. This principle did not guarantee the most meaningful view, just the most pessimistic. Given that most investments have tended to rise in value over the years balance sheets often contained hidden value but the book keeping was easy – none was needed.

The latest direction is towards showing investments at market value. This gives a better understanding of the resources which the organisation can make use of.

Either way you need to establish and set out the value of the investments at the year-end. A copy of the appropriate date's 'Financial Times' is worth buying to do this.

If market value goes above cost, the increase in value forms part of the total change in the value of net assets for the year. However, until you sell the investment, the gain is 'unrealised'. The gain is 'realised' if and when you sell at the higher price.

Example: 500 shares cost £2 each last year
Market value at: 31/12/(last yr) £2
31/12/(this yr) £3
(See figure 44 for Journal entries.)

(This year) Journal entries

Dr Shares	£500	
Cr Gain on Exempt Fund shares		£500

Figure 44

The gain could either be shown separately in the Income and Expenditure account, or in an additional 'statement of investment gains and losses' (see figure 45).

(This year) Balance Sheet

Investments
500 Exempt Fund shares at market value £1500

Figure 45

Producing the Final Trial Balance

At this stage you can add across the page to bring in all the adjustments you have entered. This gives you a balances list, of debits and credits, which should add to nil at the bottom. Head up another pair of columns to the right and transfer each of the balances either to 'Balance sheet' or to 'I&E'. The balances go into one or the other. Going back to basics should help you get this right. What is the account made up of?

assets and liabilities – balance sheet
income or expense – I & E

What you will find is that the Debits/Credits in the Income and Expenditure section are unequal. With luck, the same should be true of the Balance Sheet, for the same amount. The reason, and the difference, is the surplus or deficit for the year. If the credits are bigger than the debits in the I & E columns you have a surplus. If debits exceed credits it is a deficit. Enter the difference right at the bottom so that the total is nil. Then enter it again in the balance sheet with the opposite sign (i.e. if it is a debit in the I & E it should be a credit in the balance sheet).

Your framework is now complete. All you have to do is decide how to lay it out.

Checking the Story

Before you go on to the detailed lay-out of your accounts, check that what you have makes sense. You started off with a receipts and payments summary which gave you a figure for the change in cash during the year. How does that compare with the surplus or deficit that your final trial balance shows? Starting with that cash change, jot down the reasons why the 'surplus' or 'deficit' is different. A rough schedule might read as per figure 46.

Increase in cash for the year			£600
Add:	insurance paid year in advance	£250	
	oil stock increase over last year	100	
			350
Less:	Depreciation charge for year	500	
	Increase in accruals	400	
			(900)
Surplus shown in trial balance			£50

Figure 46 Rough schedule of surplus/deficit

Next, look at the Balance Sheet. Are the values shown correct? Are there any assets which are stated at a value higher or lower than they are really worth? Are the liabilities at what you will have to pay to settle them? Is anything missing?

Drafting the Accounts

The accounts will be made up of:

1. 'Income and expenditure account' or 'statement of trans-

actions' that shows what has happened during the year.

2. 'Balance sheet' or 'statement of affairs' that shows the assets, liabilities and funds.

3. Possibly a statement that shows the cash flow for the period. At the time of writing there is no proposal to make cash flow statements compulsory for charities unless they meet 2 out of 3 of:

Income of over £2.8 million
Balance sheet total of over £1.4 million
More than 50 employees

The design and content of cash flow statements is governed by Financial Reporting Standard 1, 'Cash Flow Statements.' If you simply want to convey the facts of what happened to the cash position, you could include the receipts and payments account as a supplementary note to the accounts.

4. An explanation of the accounting policies used.

5. Details of movements of any individual funds.

6. Other notes which will help readers of the accounts to understand what has happened. Schedules of fixed assets and investments, if you have any, will be required, but the notes can be used to give blow by blow detail on any item you think needs it.

What follows is a checklist intended to help you get the message across clearly. It cannot tell you what you must do – that must be down to you to check out against the exact status of your organisation.

INCOME AND EXPENDITURE ACCOUNT

The aim is to provide most of the information that explains what resources came in, where they came from, and how they were used, onto one page.

Which items are self-explanatory? Which need more detail? Can you group the headings to emphasise the story?

Cluttering the page with a long list of small expenses that together add up to 5% of the total is a distraction from the main story. Take them as a single line on the income and expenditure account and show the list as a note.

Where the detail is to be found in a note put the note number in brackets alongside the actual figures. Do make sure that the figures in the notes and in the front sheet are the same. Getting the balance right between, at one extreme a five line income statement with ten pages of supplementary notes, and at the other, a dense list of figures with no real pattern, is a fine art.

Try to show figures gross except where there is good reason

to put them together. In all cases, even if you put the net figure into the I&E, show the gross figures in a note and clearly state the fact that the figure is net.

Fund-raising net £5567

The supporting note would give the gross takings, analysis of expenses, and the net, for each significant event.

A church's outside giving might be £2000, comprising 20 or more individual donations. Only the £2000 should go on the face of the I&E, but the full list of donations will be a valuable feature in the notes.

You need to show the previous year's equivalent figures alongside the current year. Traditionally the Income and Expenditure account ends with a 'bottom line' – the surplus or deficit for the year. Is this the most appropriate way of expressing it for your organisation? A neutral phrase like 'Change in resources' could be more meaningful. It removes the idea of success and failure. A surplus could mean that you have failed to use the money given to you to be used, say for a disaster appeal. Where you revalue items, or make profits on sale of investments, it can be helpful to show a position arising from the normal operations, followed by a statement of gains and losses arising from sales of fixed assets and revaluations.

The acid tests on any point of presentation are:

* does it make it easier to understand?
* does it conceal or reveal the underlying facts?

As long as you set out with a mission to clarify and explain you should not go too far wrong.

BALANCE SHEET OR STATEMENT OF AFFAIRS

Show separately Fixed Assets, Investments, Current Assets, Current Liabilities and Long-term Liabilities. Make clear where there are any restrictions on the use of assets. The convention for the lay-out order is shown in figure 47.

Again, keep this page as short and simple as you can. The message you are trying to convey is: here are the resources we have, and here are the obligations.

CASH FLOW STATEMENT

In the type of organisation this book is aimed at, it is unlikely that a cash flow statement will add much value to the accounts. The aim of the cash flow statement is to show what changed the cash balances as against what changed the total net assets.

A rough worksheet for you to build up your cash flow statement would be that shown in figure 48.

Fixed assets
Investments
Current assets
  Stock
  Debtors & pre-payments
  Cash
Current liabilities
Net current assets (sub total of current assets less
  current liabilities)
Long-term liabilities
Net assets (sub total of all above)
Analysis of funds

Figure 47 Lay-out for Balance Sheet or Statement of Affairs

Start point: net change in resources before revaluations: surplus/(deficit)		£xxxx
Add back: depreciation expense for the year		xxxx
Changes in current assets and liabilities		
Add increase in creditors	£ xxxx	
Less decrease in creditors	(xxxx)	
Add decrease in stock	xxxx	
Less increase in stock	(xxxx)	
Add decrease in debtors	xxxx	
Less increase in debtors	(xxxx)	
		xxxx
Net cash flow from operating activities		xxxx
Purchase of fixed assets	(xxxx)	
Sale of fixed assets	xxxx	
Purchase of investments	(xxxx)	
Sale of investments	xxxx	
Net cash flow from investing activities		xxxx
Total net cash flow		xxxx
Cash at beginning of year	xxxx	
Cash at end of year	xxxx	
Net cash flow		xxxx

Figure 48 Rough worksheet for building up a Cash Flow Statement

ACCOUNTING POLICIES

Set out the policies used to account for:

a) how and when you recognise different types of income – donations, grants, legacies, dividends, income tax refunds etc
b) the basis of valuation of stocks, investments and other assets
c) how you deal with unrealised gains on revaluation if you carry assets at market value
d) capitalisation and depreciation.

ADDITIONAL COSTS

Fixed assets should be analysed for each separate category. Freehold buildings, leasehold buildings, fixtures and fittings, office equipment, motor vehicles.

	£
Cost or valuation	
Opening balance	xxxx
Additions in the year	xxxx
Revaluations	xxxx
Disposals	xxxx
Closing balance	xxxx
Accumulated Depreciation	
Opening balance	xxxx
Charge for year	xxxx
Disposals	xxxx
Closing balance	xxxx
Net Book Value	
At end of year	xxxx
At start of year	xxxx

Figure 49 Analysis of fixed assets

A useful addition would be a straight list that showed

a) what the asset is
b) what it cost
c) its latest net book value
d) how much it would cost to replace

e) roughly when it will need replacing
   e.g. next year
   next two years
   next five years

Investments also need a back-up note. It should show:
What the investment is and the holding.
What it cost.
Market value last year.
Market value this year.
I also prefer to underline the value at which it is carried in the accounts (see figure 50).

	Cost	Market Value 31/12 this year	Market Value 31/12 last year
CBF Investment Fund 11456 shares	50578	64147	53642

Figure 50 Back up note for investments

FUNDS

If you have a series of separate special funds the key information people need to understand is:
What is their purpose?
How much are they worth?
What assets make them up?
What restrictions exist on their use?
What happened to them in the year?
Income
Expenditure
Transfers to and from other funds.

Legislation and Statements of Recommended Practice

Ensuring that your accounts comply with an ever changing legal and regulatory framework is tough, and not a task where common sense and a willing heart will do. Even if your organisation is not covered by any regulations you probably need an up to date qualified accountant to confirm that is the case. My recommendation has to be:

1. Prepare your presentation to the point where you believe it

gives a full and accurate picture of the transactions for the year and the status at the end of the year.
2. Ask a professional to go through it with you and ensure that the accounts comply with the latest legal requirements and any professional guidances.

The Treasurer's Report

The accounts are finished to the best of your ability. Surely the figures speak for themselves? They do not. My experience is that the vast majority of members of any voluntary organisation do not understand the accounts, and are too embarrassed to say so, or ask questions at the A.G.M. Too often that suits the management committee, and the Treasurer, just fine. They read fearful acquiescence as silent support.

I am asking you to walk the extra mile, to write a report that tells the story of the year and says where you are financially. Your greatest asset could be that, although you have learnt enough about accounting jargon to do the job, you can still remember how to speak and write in plain English.

What was good?
What went well?
What went wrong?
What do we need to do?
What are we going to do?

You might even get a question to answer.

11
THE AUDIT

Roles

The auditor's job is to ensure that the accounts give an honest and correct picture of what has happened and the financial position at the accounting date. To do that he needs to examine your records, and to understand how the organisation works, especially the kind of controls in place to prevent things going wrong.

The biggest part of his job, though, will be checking your records. Your objective is to make his job as easy as possible.

Audit File

An audit file is not a plastic bag which has everything in it, somewhere. All the contents should be clearly labelled and secure, not waiting to tumble into a heap at the first opportunity. I give my ideal list below.

ACCOUNTS FILE

Two copies of this year's accounts and one copy of last year's.

Extended trial balance from which the accounts are prepared.

Wherever the entry in the accounts is made up of several items on the trial balance, a schedule showing the list of individual items. It must add up.

Journal entries.

Working papers which show how the journal entries were calculated, including copies of invoices and any supporting correspondence.

CASH BOOK FILE

Cash book with payments and receipts vouchers in sequence. Where there is no voucher, make that clear – it will save the auditor's time looking for it.

Bank statements in sequence. If you lost one, write to the bank for a replacement before the audit.

CORRESPONDENCE & MINUTES FILE
A full set of minutes in date order.
Copies of any reports you have produced during the year.
Any letters that you have written or received.

ORGANISATION FILE
Names, addresses and telephone numbers of all other people involved in processes which relate to the accounts – Membership Secretary, event organisers, Bookings Secretary, Stewardship Secretary. The auditor may need to consult or check their records as supporting evidence for yours.

Timetable and Plan

'Here are the books. It's all there. The A.G.M.'s next week.' No. Prepare a timetable, in discussion with the auditor, that works backwards from the A.G.M. date.

Get firm dates in both your diaries for:

- a handover briefing where you take him through the shape of the files and tell him of any items that concern you
- a mid-audit session to discuss problems. This gives you some leverage to make sure that the audit is actually under way.
- a final discussion of the accounts and any matters which the auditor wants to discuss. This one might well include other committee members.

Final Accounts

Do not jump the gun on producing the accounts. Regard them as draft, capable of being changed, until the audit is complete. You should then get the committee to approve them. The auditor may also ask for a 'letter of representation' where the committee certify to the auditor that voluntary income has all been recorded, or that the amount included as a provision for the settlement of a dispute over the lighting contract is reasonable.

Keeping a Good Auditor

Take him seriously. Listen to recommendations he has for change and discuss them positively. Nothing gives an auditor more pleasure than seeing something wrong put right, or a good idea taken up.

Finally, even an honorary audit is worth a tangible thank you. He can always donate the bottle to the next raffle.

Appendix 1

STARTING FROM SCRATCH

How do you go about organising the finances as Treasurer for a brand new voluntary organisation?

Sources of Help

OTHER TREASURERS

The organisation you are helping to start may be unique in some way. It will also have things in common with many others. The local library will have details of a mass of voluntary organisations and contact names. Make a few phone calls to those that sound close to what you want to do and ask to be put in touch with the Treasurer. Half an hour looking at how he keeps his books, a copy of his accounts, and a discussion on how his group works, should give you some ideas, even if it is only how not to do it.

BANK

Whatever you do, you need a bank account. Shop around. Some banks now provide information packs and special services for clubs and voluntary organisations.

NATIONAL ORGANISATIONS PROVIDING INFORMATION AND SUPPORT

Charity Commission
St Alban's House, 57/60 Haymarket, London SW1Y 4QX
Guidance leaflets available free. Very well informed staff. If you are intending to operate as a charity, this should be your first call.

National Council for Voluntary Organisations (NCVO)
26 Bedford Square, London WC1B 3HU
Publish a range of books and booklets written specifically for voluntary organisations.

Directory of Social Change
Radius Works, Back Lane, London NW3 1HL
Publish books, booklets and run affordable training courses.

UNDERSTANDING THE RULES

Good causes are covered by the law, and tax. The 1992 Charities Act is covered by a Charity Commission booklet. Tax law affecting voluntary organisations is far from simple. There is a widespread belief that, if you are doing something for charity, you do not have to worry about tax. That is completely untrue. Income tax, VAT, PAYE and National Insurance are all potential nightmares. You need to understand at least the basic rules.

The Inland Revenue has a separate section for charities.

Inland Revenue Claims Branch
Charity Division, St John's House, Merton Road, Bootle, Merseyside, L69 9BB.
Supply a valuable 'charity tax pack'.

Other people to consult are:

Customs & Excise (VAT)
Trading Standards Department
Local Council

OTHER USEFUL ORGANISATIONS

Charities Aid Foundation
48 Pembury Road, Tonbridge, TN9 2JD
Administer covenant schemes for charities and provide investment facilities.

Charities Official Investment Fund
St Alphage House, 2 Fore Street, London EC2Y 5AQ
Provide a range of investment facilities for charities.

Expertise

Reading the leaflets and booklets above will make you acquainted with the problems you and the organisation have to deal with. It will not make you an expert, nor will this book.

It is vital to understand when you need expert advice. As a trustee – and, whether you use that title or not, you probably are one – you are personally liable for failure to exercise due standards of care. Exercising due standards of care includes getting expert advice when you need it. Ignorance is no defence.

Try to get access to local experts, perhaps on a limited basis rather than asking them to sit on the committee. The list could include:

Solicitor
Chartered/Certified Accountant
Insurance Broker
Architect/surveyor

If you decide that you are prepared to buy these services, do look for proof of relevant expertise and accomplishment. Discuss this with other local Treasurers. Where do they go for advice? How pleased are they with the service?

Is It Really Necessary?

Before you rush off to clear all the hurdles involved in setting up a new club or charity, are you sure that you need to? The administration will tie up effort and skill that could be used to good effect elsewhere, perhaps raising funds for a charity that already exists and is short of support, or helping breathe new life into a similar club. The actual expenses that show up in the accounts for cost of administration are minimal compared to the value of time and effort used up. You might even avoid taking on the Treasurer's job.

Appendix 2

EXPLANATORY NOTES ON ACCOUNTING JARGON

Conventions

USE OF BRACKETS ( )

In the presentation of accounts, brackets are generally used instead of a minus sign. However, it is not an entirely logical system – in order to keep the appearance reasonable it is not normal to show a list of expenditure with brackets round each number.

If it is not absolutely clear what the brackets mean in a particular situation it is helpful to show this in the text. 'Surplus/(deficit)' means, 'If there are no brackets it is a surplus, if there are brackets it is a deficit.'

In double entry book-keeping brackets are used to signify 'credits'.

BOXES

Putting a box around a group of numbers in a column shows that those numbers are to be added together. The sum will be the number directly under the box. Another method is to offset the group of numbers to be added in a separate column to the left. Boxes can be handy if you are short of columns and can be clearer to understand.

Accounting Concepts

Bases, concepts, principles: all these boil down to the framework of thinking used to prepare accounts.

ACCRUALS CONCEPT

If the boiler repair was done just before the end of the year, and the invoice arrived too late to write a cheque in the year, the 'accruals' concept says that you should include the cost of that invoice in the old year's accounts. If a committee member sells 20 tickets for a New Year's Eve dance at £5 each, and forgets to bring the cash with him on the night, but confirms that he has, and owes, that amount, the 'accruals' concept says that you should include that £100 in the accounts of the dance, and of the year.

You can also think of it as 'matching' the income and expense together, making sure that the period shows all the costs that relate to it but *only* the costs that relate to it. It ignores when the cash moves and asks what period it relates to. When was the income earned? When was the work done?

It may help just to see 'accruals' as the opposite of receipts and payments. See figure 51 for examples.

Amounts shown in accounts ending 31/12	Receipts & Payments Basis	Accruals Basis
a) £500 insurance premium paid by cheque 20/12 for next year's cover	£500	nil
b) £250 gas bill for gas used in the quarter ended November. Cheque paid the following January.	nil	£250
c) £2500 photocopier bought 1/1. It is expected to last 5 years, and to be scrapped for nothing at the end.	£2500	£500 (per year)
d) £200 rent due for last quarter. Received 2/1 the following year.	nil	£200

Figure 51 Accruals may be seen as the opposite of receipts and payments

GOING CONCERN CONCEPT

'Going concern' means you prepare the accounts on the basis that the organisation is going to continue, that it does not have to be closed down and everything sold off. If you hold stationery stock worth £200 at cost, and you are absolutely certain that it will be used normally, it stays at £200. If you had to sell up tomorrow it might well be worth less. 'Going concern', as long as the organisation is healthy and able to continue, says that you do not need to use a 'firesale' approach to valuing things.

CONSISTENCY CONCEPT

One year's accounts should be prepared on the same basis as the next. When a member looks at this year's figures compared to last year's it should be a fair comparison. If a change has been made to the way something is handled, the change should be explained, and the effects of that change explained clearly. For example, if you switched from 'receipts and payments' to 'accruals', you would re-calculate last year's accounts on the accruals basis as well, and highlight where it made a difference.

There is a strong moral undercurrent to this concept. Changes should be made only to improve understanding and presentation. They should be carefully considered.

PRUDENCE CONCEPT

Prudence is the trump concept. The wedding fee was £125. They had the choir and the bells. So far the cheque has bounced three times and the churchwarden was threatened and sworn at when he tried to talk to the happy couple. Accruals says count the £125 – it was earned in the period. Prudence asks if you are reasonably certain of getting your money. If not, don't count on it. Prudence trumps accruals. Be on the gloomy side of realistic, not optimistic, when you prepare the accounts.

It is prudence that says value your stock at the lower end of what you paid for it and what you can sell it for. If your investments go down in value below their cost, the prudence concept tells you to show their new, low value, in the accounts. Finally, if something has happened today that will cost money tomorrow, take the costs into account now.

CONCEPTS ROUND UP

Apart from using the four concepts in your own thinking, understanding their rough meaning will help in discussions with qualified accountants. The concepts are part of the accounting language.

Accounting Terms

Many words carry slightly different meanings when you come across them in sets of accounts than when you deal with them in their everyday sense. I have tried to explain the most common, although in some cases the explanation of one word makes most sense when you have come to grips with a whole family of terms.

ASSETS

Items of value that the organisation owns. There are several categories, not all exclusive.

Fixed assets: usually something held to be used in the longer term (land, buildings, lawn mowers, photo-copiers, cars). The nuance of 'fixed' is that it is bought to be used rather than as stock to re-sell.

Current assets: things which are capable of being turned into cash in the short term. Originally it referred to those things which were part of the trading cycle – stocks of goods for sale, debtors, and cash when the debtors pay up. It also covers payments in advance and pre-payments.

Debtors: amounts of money owed to you and the people who owe it.

Pre-payments and payments in advance: amounts which you have paid out which have not yet been 'earned' by the other party. The classic example is an insurance premium paid in advance.

Liquid assets: those assets which can be turned into cash quickly. 'Liquidity' is the ability to be turned into cash. All liquid assets are current. Not all current assets are liquid.

Investments: stocks, shares, gilt edged securities, unit trusts, war loan are all examples of investments. Items held to provide income and/or growth in value, rather than to be used. Investments can also be land and buildings, or antiques. They can be either fixed (e.g. land held for long term investment) or current. Whether they are 'fixed' or 'current', the best course is to show them separately under their own heading.

ASSET VALUATION

Historic cost: what you paid for them when you bought them. The figure in the cash book.

Market value: used mainly for investments that are 'quoted'. If the investment is listed each day in the *Daily Telegraph* or *Financial Times* you could refer to the price quoted there as the 'market value'.

Open market value: not really an accounting term, but it means the price you would get if you sold openly, say at auction. It could also be used fairly to describe the estimated value of a piece of land, or a building.

Net realisable value: what you think you could sell it for. Net realisable value is used when you are looking at stock, office equipment and the like.

Carrying value: the value at which an asset is shown in the accounts.

Inflation, wear and tear, obsolescence, technology changes, all these affect the value of assets over time. The balance sheet adds up, but whether it makes sense (or gives a true and fair view) depends on whether the values stated make sense. The thinking has changed towards stating fixed assets and investments at their market value, so that each year's results contain and show the effects of value changes as well as income and expense.

Where does this leave you? Recognise that cost and value are not necessarily the same thing. Find out, or estimate, for any material assets, what they are worth – the market value. Make sure that your accounts explain to members what the assets are, what basis is used to value them and what they are worth. The current guidance on valuation rules is:

Fixed assets	– Cost or valuation, less depreciation.
Investments	– Cost or market value. If market value is lower than cost, then the market value must be used.
Current assets	– the lower of cost and net realisable value.
Liabilities	– what it will cost to settle them.

CAPITAL (AND CAPITAL EXPENDITURE)

Capital, in phrases like 'venture capital', 'raising capital' and even 'capitalist', means the money invested in a business. There is another meaning, closer to the idea expressed in 'capital ships' (the biggest battleships). A 'capital' item is something of material value which is purchased for long term use. If that sounds like 'fixed asset', it should, because it is. The distinction and judgement you have to make is between capital and expense. The difference it makes is in how much gets charged to the accounts in the year.

By 'capitalising' an asset you:

a) spread the cost over the period it is used (its 'useful life')
b) record the fact that the organisation owns something and what it is worth.

It can simplify matters if you have a 'capital' limit, £50, £100, or higher, below which you regard any expenditure as expense.

Otherwise you can have pointless philosophical debates over the useful life of a £1 biro or a £20 toilet seat.

DEPRECIATION (also amortisation or writing down)

The reduction in value of a fixed asset over time, caused by use, wear and tear, obsolescence, etc. A car is a good example. It depreciates, or loses value, from the day it is put on the road until the day it is scrapped. The depreciation charge, or expense, for the year should be the amount by which it has lost value in the year. For convenience the depreciation charge is usually calculated evenly (straight line).

Example:

Car bought for £12,000. Estimated life 5 years. Estimated value at the end of 5 years £2,000.

At the end of the first year the accounts would show:

In the Balance sheet

Fixed assets	Car	cost	£12,000
	Less	depreciation	(2,000)
		net book value	10,000

In the Income & Expenditure account

	Depreciation expense	2,000

Other phrases you may come across are:

Writing down: reducing the value in the books, almost identical with depreciating, but also covers reflecting the loss in value of investments or stock.

Net book value: the value of the asset in the books after deducting depreciation.

Written down value: as for net book value but you might use this phrase in preference when describing the value of investments.

Revaluation: generally used when you decide that an asset is stated at too low a value. Adjusting the value of an asset in the books to reflect its latest market value. For quoted investments this is straightforward. For land or buildings you would need to explain who had valued them and on what basis.

If you stick to receipts and payments format for your accounts, you do not need to keep a formal account of capital and depreciation. A voluntary organisation may well work on the basis of fund-raising to pay for any large capital items, and feel that it is then paid for and done with. However, the recommended practice is that you should capitalise and depreciate fixed assets except in three cases:

1) where the asset is 'inalienable' (i.e. you actually have no

say over what is done with it and could not dispose of it even if you wanted to)
2) where the asset is historic (e.g. an ancient monument)
3) where no-one knows either what it cost or what it is worth.

Even if you decide not to capitalise, you would still need to state what fixed assets there are, and how much they are worth. It is part of the wide financial picture – what do you own, what is it worth and when will it need replacement? In fact you might well go beyond the information given by looking at what the assets you already have cost when you bought them, and estimate what they would cost to replace today.

LIABILITIES

Amounts of money which you owe. Amounts which are due to be repaid within one year of the accounting date are *current* liabilities. Amounts due to be repaid later than one year from the accounting date are *deferred* liabilities. They should be shown separately. The point of this is that, when someone looks at the balance sheet, they can work out your immediate financial health by comparing your current assets with your current liabilities. Examples of liabilities are creditors, loans, bank overdraft, provisions, accruals.

Creditors: anyone who has provided goods or services which you have not paid for – the gas board, fire extinguisher service company, stationery suppliers. The amounts making up creditors would usually be a list of unpaid invoices.

Loans: money lent to the organisation.

Accruals: basically a creditor who has not invoiced you yet, or a calculation of the part of a bill which relates to the period you are dealing with. An accrual is an estimate of what you owe.

Provision: an estimated amount set aside to cover a liability or a loss in value. Where you believe that you owe money, but you cannot estimate with any certainty how much it is, you could make a provision in the accounts for the rough amount which you think you may end up paying. This comes down to bad news that you want to reflect as soon as you know about it. By tradition the full title of the value of depreciation in the balance sheet is 'provision for depreciation'. If you decide that there is a problem over collecting money owed to you, you might take a 'provision for doubtful debt'. If you decide that some stock cannot be realised for what it cost you take a 'provision for stock loss'.

The difference between an accrual and a provision lies in the extent of uncertainty and the sense of anticipating bad news.

FUND

The net value of the assets and liabilities of the operation. What the club is worth. The figure that makes the balance sheet add up. 'Funds' in lay language means amounts of money, possibly put on one side. 'How much is in the fund?' is usually asking how much cash there is. The question that 'fund' answers in a set of accounts is, 'How much is there if all the assets are sold at their stated values and all the liabilities are paid off?'. Where it is vital is in understanding the restrictions that exist on using cash and assets. Recognising different funds usually involves understanding how some things are earmarked.

General fund

The choir have £500 in the bank. They own no other assets and have no creditors. There are no conditions on what they can do with the cash. The Choir Fund, or Choir General Fund will be £500 also.

Designated fund

The choir choose to put half their cash on one side for the organist to spend on music. It is their choice, and they could later decide to use it for something else. They therefore transfer £250 from the General Fund to the Music Fund. The Music Fund is a designated fund. The balance sheet now reads:

Cash	£500
Represented by:	
Choir General Fund	£250
Choir Music Fund	£250
	£500

Restricted Fund

In the new year the choir decides to buy new robes. They make an appeal for donations, specifying that the money given will only be used for robes. £750 is donated. They can now only use this money for robes, otherwise they will be in breach of trust. The £750 will therefore make up a restricted fund. Even when the robes are bought, any money left over will have to stay in that fund.

Cash	£1250
Represented by:	
Choir General Fund	£250
Choir Music Fund	£250

Choir Robes Fund	£750
	£1250

'The general fund and music fund are unrestricted. The robes fund may only be used for the purpose of purchasing and maintaining choir robes.'

A restricted fund could also be set up by a donor making conditions as to the use of the asset at the time of donation. It is therefore very important to keep track of the exact status of the different funds. On a practical level, if you appeal for money for a specific purpose, it can be useful to add a rider that says surplus cash will also be used for other things. If a project comes up which meets the terms of cash you hold in a restricted fund, it is usually sensible to use the restricted fund money first, in preference to general fund money.

BALANCE SHEET OR STATEMENT OF AFFAIRS

The balance sheet used to be a list of balances, mostly at historic cost. The individual parts might or might not give an up to date picture of the organisation's worth. Most changes in accounting rules recently have been directed towards making the balance sheet a more accurate and up to date picture. Rather than worry about the technical detail, set out with your statement of affairs to communicate clearly:

* what you own and use and what it is worth
* what you owe
* what restrictions there are on what you can do with it.

It still has to add up, but remember that it is there for a purpose, not just as a pretty schedule.

OTHER TERMS

Commitment

A legal obligation, a contract to purchase equipment or services in the future.

The balance sheet will show assets and liabilities at the accounting date. It is also important to explain what future obligations exist. If you have cash of £10,000, but signed a contract for the building of a new clubhouse costing £100,000, with the work due to start in the New Year, then the accounts will not give a complete view unless you include a note on the 'commitment'. Another example would be a photocopier ordered in December and due to be installed in January, if the order was binding.

Material

Important, significant, big. Something which, if missed out or wrongly stated, would make the accounts not give a true and fair view. This is very much a matter of context and judgement. The £50 accrual for gas used but not invoiced could be materially correct if it was within £20 of the right figure. The cash at bank figure needs to be spot on. A £100 error that made the accounts show a surplus instead of a deficit could be material and need correction. A £100 error against a £35,600 surplus would probably not be. Materiality is also about not cluttering the page with a welter of small figures when you could group them and get some focus on what they mean.

Anything the Treasurer wants to hide that the auditor finds.

Immaterial

Unimportant, insignificant, small. Even if you got it hopelessly wrong the accounts would tell the same story and be true and fair. Anything the Treasurer wants to hide, like the bank charges he should have avoided or the petty cash discrepancy.

Forecast: guess as to what will happen.

Scientifically based forecast: guess covered in bullshit.

Realised and Unrealised

Realised means turned into hard cash, in the bag. If your investments go up in value you have a potential, or unrealised, profit. When you sell them for cash you have a 'realised' profit.

True and Fair View

Depending on the nature and size of the organisation, the auditor may be required to report on whether the accounts give a 'true and fair view' of the financial activities and the state of affairs. There ought to be a definition of what this means. There is not. The accounting profession have developed a series of 'Statements of Standard Accounting Practice' (SSAP's), 'Financial Reporting Standards' (FRS's), 'Statements of Recommended Practice' (SORP's) and 'Urgent Issues Task Force Consensus Pronouncements' (UITF's). They set out principles, rules and guidances as to how accounts should be prepared and what they should reflect. Increasingly the 'standards' are acquiring legal force.

Complying with all of these instructions and guidances ought to mean that your accounts give a 'true and fair view' but there is room for judgement, and the development of standards and guidances is continuous. This is an area to take expert advice. Before you spend money, try one of the support organisations listed in Appendix 1. This minefield is reason enough in itself to get a practising qualified accountant onto the team.

Appendix 3

DOUBLE ENTRY BOOK KEEPING

Introduction

The idea of this appendix is to provide some theory and examples of accounting entries. It follows the increasingly complex history of the completely fictional Najafabad Cricket Club as it develops towards first class status. Cricket clubs in Persia in the 1890's pay no tax and do not have to cope with VAT. Pounds are purely a convention and nothing approaching similarity to any institution actually in existence is intended.

The method of writing journal entries out onto an extended trial balance, described in Chapter 6 and exemplified here, is one which I have found to work, and to be understandable to novices. The end result is a document that contains all the entries for the year. From it a traditional income and expenditure account and balance sheet can be prepared. This may not be the appropriate or required form for your accounts, but it is a sound starting point to work from.

1. THEORY

Double entry is logical, but understanding seems to come as a revelation, often after long straining.

Every transaction has two aspects – a debit and a credit. Dr and Cr for short.

Debits are:

* assets
* expenses
* losses

Credits are:

* liabilities
* income
* profits

By tradition, debits go on the left and credits go on the right.

Also by tradition, if you do not use left and right, debits are positive numbers and credits have brackets round (or minus signs in front).

Use cash as your start point to understanding. Cash is an asset. Assets are debits. Therefore cash in hand is a debit balance. A cash receipt increases cash held. It debits cash, thus making the debit balance bigger, so the other side of the entry must be a credit. The other side of receiving cash would be:

a) it is a loan that you still owe
b) it is some form of income which you can keep.

A cash payment is a credit to cash. It reduces the balance in hand. If it is a credit to cash, the other side of the entry must be a debit. The other side of a cash payment could be:

a) a loan to someone, who is therefore your debtor
b) an expense
c) the purchase of some kind of asset – stock or equipment.

At this point try very hard to detach yourself from any philosophical notion of debits or credits being good or bad things. It is just a way of recording financial transactions that works. One way of remembering it is that the entries in the cash book are always the wrong way round because they are the other side of the entry.

If the memory of your bank statement haunts your thinking, remember it is because it is the bank's cash book, not yours.

Some simple examples:

1. Purchase ten rolls of toilet paper and pay by cheque.

		Dr	Cr
Dr	hall consumables expense	£5	
Cr	cash		£5

2. Purchase a piece of land and pay by cheque.

		Dr	Cr
Dr	land (asset)	£50,000	
Cr	cash		£50,000

3. Collect subscriptions.

		Dr	Cr
Dr	Cash	£200	
Cr	Subscriptions income		£200

This way of writing down the transaction is a journal entry. By convention, the debit entry always comes first and is set slightly to the left. If you make no mistakes the sum total of your debits will always equal the sum total of your credits.

2. NAJAFABAD CRICKET CLUB

The year is 1890. Influenced by a wandering English archaeologist, a group of twenty Persians get together to form the Najafabad Cricket Club. They decide to donate £50 each to get the club off the ground. The Treasurer collects the cash, buys a cash book for £5 and opens a bank account. Nothing else happens before the end of the year.

The transactions for the year as detailed in the cash book are shown in figure 52.

Receipts		Payments	
Donations	£1000	Stationery	£ 5
		Balance carried down	995
	£1000		£1000
Balance brought down	995		

Figure 52 Transactions for the year as detailed in the Cash Book

More convention. If the account is prepared in this way, to work out the balance you add up both sides separately. Enter the difference on the side with the smaller figure (balance carried down). Both sides now add up to the same figure. Rule off and enter the difference on the opposite side below the total (balance brought down).

Abbreviations and different forms are:

Balance carried down	Bal c/d
Balance carried forward	Bal c/fwd
Balance brought down	Bal b/d
Balance brought forward	Bal b/fwd

One reason to make do without a formal ledger is to avoid spending the best years of your life ruling neat lines and writing Bal c/d for no real benefit.

For the more mathematical or computer minded you can visualise a single column with pluses for debits and minuses for credits. The 'balance' of the account will be the net of all the individual entries.

In the 'ledger', if we had one, there would be two pages (see figure 53).

The same could be represented on different paper (see figure 54).

You could buy a bound book or a lever arch file, open an account on a fresh page for each heading of income or expense and make the opposite entries when you write up the cash

Donations			
	Dr		Cr
		Cash book	£1000

Stationery			
	Dr		Cr
Cash book	£5		

Figure 53

Donations		
	Dr	Cr
Cash book		£1000

Stationery		
	Dr	Cr
Cash book	£5	

Figure 54

book. In practice this is not necessary. The analysis columns in the cash book are your shorthand ledger. If there are only a few adjustments to make you can use a single sheet of paper to act as the whole ledger for the year. You just need to remember that the columns in the payments analysis are debits and those on the receipts analysis are credits, and this only when you come to prepare the accounts at the end of the year.

During the year, concentrate on using the cash book and the cash balance to understand, and let others know, where you are. The single sheet of paper is an 'extended trial balance'. To start though, the trial balance is just a list of all the balances.

The trial balance would read as per figure 55.

	Dr	Cr
Cash at bank	£ 995	
Stationery	5	
Donations		£1000
	£1000	£1000

Figure 55 Trial balance

To produce the accounts we need to consider what each of the balances is:
The cash at bank is an asset. It goes in the balance sheet.
The stationery is expense – there is no intention of selling the cash book, just using it. It goes in the income and expenditure account.
The donations are income. They also go to the income and expenditure account.
The accounts would now read as per figure 56.

Najafabad Cricket Club
Income and expenditure account
for the year ended 31/12/1890

Income		
Donations		£1000
Less:		
Expense – stationery		5
Surplus for the year		995
Balance sheet as at 31.12.1890		
Cash at bank		995
Represented by:		
Club fund		
Balance b/fwd 1.1.1890	nil	
Surplus for the year	£995	
Balance c/fwd 31.12.1890		£995

Figure 56 The accounts

Finally the opening trial balance for the new year would be as figure 57.

	Dr	Cr
Cash at bank	£ 995	
Club fund		£995
	£995	£995

Figure 57 Opening trial balance for the new year

The club fund is a credit balance. In a sense this means that the 'club' is owed or entitled to the total asset value, in this case, the cash. Another way to think about it is that the club fund is the cumulative sum of all the surpluses made and profits are credits, so that means the club fund ought to be a credit.

3. 1891

In 1891 the members set an annual membership fee at £10, buy a square of desert, and start to play matches. Their enthusiasm is matched only by the absence of opposition.

The cash book is shown in figure 58.

All bills have been paid at the end of the year and all the subscriptions are in. Prepare the accounts.

1. Work out the cash balance: £1427 − £915 = £512.

2. Review the payments and decide which are expenses, which assets. Use the 'matching' concept. Which items should be matched just with 1891 and which are longer term?

The land will be saleable at any time and changes in value will probably not be related to the use it gets as a cricket pitch. It may change in value but will not wear out.

The equipment will probably last two or three seasons. As it is lots of small items you decide to treat it as expense of the year.

3. Write up the journal. This is just a traditional name for the book or piece of paper you use to record accounting entries. Strictly the cash book entries do not need to be recorded in a journal because the cash book is part of the accounts. I find it helps keep a clear record to schedule out the cash book entries for the year as a journal.

4. Work out the extended trial balance. This is a way of getting the whole of the accounts onto one piece of paper. The snag is that you need a wide piece of paper, or two sheets of A4 taped together or a spare page of the cash book.

1891 Cash Book Payments

5/1/91	S Shah land purchase	£650
6/3/91	A Baligh cricket equipment	60
6/4/91	S Yektai balls	10
2/7/91	Umpire fees	10
2/7/91	B Samanianpur barbecue food	25
2/7/91	Y Ghodooshim barn dance caller	25
2/8/91	Umpire fees	10
15/12/91	A Baligh medals	25
15/12/91	B Samanianpur annual dinner expenses	100
	Total payments	£915

1891 Cash Book Receipts

Balance brought forward 1/1/91		£995
30/1/91	Subscriptions	220
2/7/91	Barbecue & barn dance tickets	90
2/7/91	Match fees	11
2/8/91	Match fees	11
15/12/91	Annual dinner tickets	100
	Total receipts (incl b/fwd balance)	£1427

Figure 58 The Cash Book

Across the top, from left to right, you need columns for

1. Account name
2. Opening balances Dr
3. Opening balances Cr
4. Cash book entries Dr
5. Cash book entries Cr
6. Journals Dr
7. Journals Cr
8. Balances — Use brackets to show credits.
9. Income and expenditure — "
10. Balance sheet — "

Start by entering the opening balances (see figure 59).

Next summarise the cash book payments and receipts for the year, as shown in figure 60.

Najafabad Cricket Club
Extended Trial Balance 31.12.1891

Account	Opening Balance Dr	Opening Balance Cr
Cash at bank	£995	
Fund b/fwd		£995

Figure 59 Opening balances for the Extended Trial Balance

Najafabad Cricket Club
Extended Trial Balance 31.12.1891

Account	Opening Balance Dr	Opening Balance Cr	Cash Book Dr	Cash Book Cr
Cash at bank	£995		£432	£915
Fund b/fwd		£995		
Subscriptions				220
Match fees				22
Fund-raising income				90
Dinner			100	100
Land			650	
Equipment			70	
Fees			20	
Fund-raising expenses			50	
Medals			25	
	£995	£995	£1347	£1347

Figure 60 Summary of Cash Book payments and receipts for the Extended Trial Balance

The journal entries to summarise the cash book would be as shown in figure 61.

	Dr	Cr
(yr)/J1		
Dr Cash at bank	£432	
Cr Subscriptions		£220
Match fees		22
Fund-raising income		90
Dinner		100
	£432	£432
Cash receipts for 1891		
(yr)/J2		
Dr Dinner expenses	£100	
Land	650	
Equipment	70	
Fees	20	
Fund-raising expenses	50	
Medals	25	
Cr Cash at bank		£915
	£915	£915
Cash payments for 1891		

Figure 61 Journal entries to summarise the Cash Book

If there are no other adjustments to be made, you then add and subtract across the page to arrive at the net balance for each account. These balances either slot into the income and expenditure account columns or into the balance sheet columns. The only tricky bit is that the income and expenditure account columns and balance sheet columns will both be out of balance. This is shown in the first trial balance example, figure 62. The difference is either the surplus or deficit for the year. Put a new line in at the bottom for 'Surplus/deficit'.

If the debits in the I & E columns are greater than the credits, it is a deficit. Enter the balancing figure as a credit in the income and expenditure column and as a debit in the balance sheet column. If the credits in the I & E columns are greater

Najafabad Cricket Club Extended Trial Balance 31/12/1891

Account	Opening Bals		Cash Book		Bals	I&E	B/sheet
	Dr	Cr	Dr	Cr			
Cash at bank	£995		£432	(£915)	£512		£512
Fund b/f		(£995)			(£995)		(£995)
Subs				(£220)	(£220)	(£220)	
Match fees				(£22)	(£22)	(£22)	
Fnd-rais			£50	(£90)	(£40)	(£40)	
Dinner			£100	(£100)			
Land			£650		£650		£650
Equip.			£70		£70	£70	
Fees			£20		£20	£20	
Medals			£25		£25	£25	
Surplus							
	£995	(£995)	£1347	(£1347)	£0	(£167)	£167

Figure 62 Extended Trial Balance

than the debits it is a surplus. Enter the balancing figure as a debit in the I & E column and as a credit in the balance sheet column. It may seem perverse logic but it does work. See the second trial balance, figure 63.

All you have to do now is lay out the accounts (see figure 64).

Surplus or deficit may not convey the truth of what has happened for a voluntary organisation. Perhaps the Treasurer put a hold on vital projects because there was not enough cash available. A 'surplus' sounds good but the truth is that fundamental objectives were not achieved. Think about which headings make most sense for your organisation, and make sure that your accounts get across the spirit and substance of what really happened.

In these accounts the biggest decision may have been the purchase of the land. This enters the balance sheet, but does not show up in the I&E at all. A brief summary of cash flow

Najafabad Cricket Club Extended Trial Balance 31/12/1891

Account	Opening Bals Dr	Opening Bals Cr	Cash Book Dr	Cash Book Cr	Bals	I&E	B/sheet
Cash at bank	£995		£432	(£915)	£512		£512
Fund b/f		(£995)			(£995)		(£995)
Subs				(£220)	(£220)	(£220)	
Match fees				(£22)	(£22)	(£22)	
Fnd-rais			£50	(£90)	(£40)	(£40)	
Dinner			£100	(£100)			
Land			£650		£650		£650
Equip.			£70		£70	£70	
Fees			£20		£20	£20	
Medals			£25		£25	£25	
Surplus						£167	(£167)
	£995	(£995)	£1347	(£1347)	£0	£0	£0

Figure 63 Completed layout for the Extended Trial Balance

would highlight this (see figure 65). Alternatively, you could publish the receipts and payments account as a note to the accounts, as set out in Chapter 9.

4. 1892

In 1892 they build a wall around the land which should last for 10 years before it needs re-building. A roller is purchased that should last 5 years. They play 3 matches this year and increase membership. They also launch an appeal for funds to build a clubhouse and invest the money raised in 1000 Anglo-Persian oil shares at £2 per share. A deposit account is opened to earn interest on the spare cash.

The cash book entries are shown in figure 66.

At the end of 1892 the deposit account stands at £420: £20 interest was received in the year. The oil shares surged in value in December and were quoted at 31st December at £5 each.

Najafabad Cricket Club
Income & Expenditure Account for year ended 31/12/1891

Income		
Subscriptions		£220
Fund-raising	£90	
Less expenses	(50)	
		40
Match fees		22
Total income		£282
Expenditure		
Equipment	70	
Umpire fees	20	
Medals	25	
Total expense		£115
Surplus for the year		£167

Balance sheet as at 31/12/1891

Fixed assets		
Land	£650	
Current assets		
Cash at bank	512	
Total assets		£1162
Represented by:		
Club fund		
Balance b/fwd 1/1/1891	£995	
Add surplus for the year	167	
Balance c/fwd 31/12/1891		£1162

Figure 64 Layout of the accounts

Najafabad Cricket Club
Cash Flow Statement for year ended 31/12/1891

Net cash inflow from operating activities	£167
Investing activities	
Purchase of land	(650)
Decrease in cash	(483)
Cash at 1/1/1891	995
Cash at 31/1/1891	512

Figure 65 Summary of cash flow to highlight the purchase of land

1892 Cash Book Payments		
5/2/92	H Hovan wall builder	£400
2/3/92	A Baligh cricket equipment	35
6/4/92	S Yektai balls	20
7/4/92	Sharifian & Co (roller)	100
2/7/92	Umpire fees	10
30/6/92	Anglo Persian oil shares	2000
2/7/92	Transfer to deposit	400
2/7/92	M Faraji quiz refreshments	40
2/8/92	Umpire fees	10
2/9/92	Umpire fees	10
15/12/92	A Baligh medals	25
15/12/92	B Samanianpur annual dinner expenses	140
	Total payments	£3190

1892 Cash Book Receipts		
Balance brought forward 1/1/92		£512
30/1/92	Subscriptions	350
24/5/92	Clubhouse appeal	2400
2/7/92	Quiz Night tickets	100
2/7/92	Match fees	11
2/8/92	Match fees	11
2/9/92	Match fees	11
15/12/92	Annual Dinner tickets	250
	Total receipts (incl b/fwd balance)	£3645

Figure 66 Cash Book entries

The club owes a separate bill for entertainment at the dinner of £50.

Prepare the journals, trial balance, and accounts for 1892 (see figures 67–72 following).

Non Cash Book Journals

		Dr	Cr
1.	Deposit account		
	Dr Deposit account	20	
	Cr Interest income		20
	Interest on deposit account for the year.		
2.	Accruals		
	Dr Annual dinner expenses	50	
	Cr Creditors		50
	Accrue for money owing re annual dinner.		
3.	Depreciation		
	Dr Depreciation expense	40	
	Cr Provision for depreciation		40
	Depreciation of the wall. One tenth of the capital value.		
	Dr Depreciation expense	10	
	Cr Provision for depreciation		10
	Depreciation for approx half year on the roller which is believed to have a five year life. Full year charge would be £20.		
4.	Revalue the oil shares		
	Dr Oil shares	3000	
	Cr Building appeal		3000
	Unrealised gain on oil shares.		

Figure 67 Non Cash Book Journals

Najafabad Cricket Club Extended Trial Balance 31/12/1892

Account	Opening Balances Dr	Opening Balances Cr	Cash Book Dr	Cash Book Cr	Journals Dr	Journals Cr	Balances	I&E	B/sheet
Cash at bank	£512		£3133	(£3190)			£455		£455
Deposit			400		£20		420		420
Fund b/f		(£1162)					(1162)		(1162)
Clubho appeal				(2400)			(2400)		(2400)
Land	650						650		650
Wall			400				400		400
Prov for Dep'n						(40)	(40)		(40)
Roller			100				100		100
Prov for Dep'n						(10)	(10)		(10)
Investments			2000		3000		5000		5000
Creditors						(50)	(50)		(50)
Subscriptions				(350)			(350)	(350)	
Match fees				(33)			(33)	(33)	
Fund-raising			40	(100)			(60)	(60)	
Dinner			140	(250)	50		(60)	(60)	
Interest Income						(20)	(20)	(20)	
Land									
Equipment			55				55	55	
Fees			30				30	30	
Medals			25				25	25	
Depreciation					50		50	50	
Surplus							0	363	(363)
Revaluation						(3000)	(3000)		(3000)
	£ 1162	(1162)	6323	(6323)	3120	(3120)	0	0	0

Figure 68 Extended trial balance

Najafabad Cricket Club
Income & Expenditure Account
for the year ended 31/12/1892

	1892	1892	1891
Income			
Subscriptions		£350	£220
Fund-raising	£100		90
Less expenses	(40)		(50)
		60	40
Annual dinner net		60	—
Interest		20	—
Match fees		33	22
Total income		523	282
Expenditure			
Equipment	55		70
Umpire fees	30		20
Medals	25		25
Depreciation	50		—
Total expense		(160)	(115)
Surplus from operations		363	167
Unrealised Gain on revaluation of investments		3000	—
Net movement of resources		£3363	£167

Figure 69 Income and Expenditure account

Balance sheet as at 31/12/1892

	1892	1892	1891
Fixed assets			
Land	£650		£650
Wall	360		
Roller	90		
		£1100	650
Investments		5000	
Current assets			
Deposit account	420		
Cash at bank	455		512
		875	512
Less current liabilities			
Creditors		(50)	—
Net current assets		825	512
Net assets		6925	1162
Represented by:			
Club general fund			
Balance b/fwd 1 Jan	1162		995
Add surplus for year	363		167
Balance c/fwd 31 Dec		1525	1162
Club building fund			
Balance b/fwd 1 Jan	—		
Appeal donation	2400		
Unrealised gain on re-valuation of investments	3000		
Balance c/fwd 31 Dec			5400
		£6925	£1162

Figure 70 Balance sheet

Cash Flow Statement for the year ended 31 December 1892

Net surplus for year from operations		£363
Add: depreciation		50
increase in creditors		50
Net cash inflow from operations		463
Cash inflow from special appeal		2400
Total cash inflow		2863
Investing activities		
Purchase of fixed assets	(500)	
Purchase of investments	(2000)	
Cash outflow from investing activities		(2500)
Increase in cash		363
Cash at 1 January 1892		512
Cash at 31 December 1892		875

Figure 71 Cash Flow statement

Notes to the accounts

Note 1: Accounting policies

These accounts are prepared on an accruals basis, which means that income and expenditure are recognised when earned rather than when cash is paid or received. Investment income will be credited on actual receipt.

Fixed assets with a cost above £100 are capitalised and written off over their estimated useful lives. They are stated at cost less depreciation.

Freehold land is not depreciated.

Investments are stated at market value as at 31st December 1892. Unrealised gains or (losses) are credited (charged) to the relevant fund.

There were no commitments outstanding at 31st December 1892.

Note 2: Fixed Assets

	Land	Wall	Machinery
Cost or valuation			
Opening balance 1 Jan	£650	–	–
Additions	–	£400	£100
Revaluations	–	–	–
Disposals	–	–	–
31 December 1892	650	400	100
Accumulated depreciation			
Opening balance for 1 Jan		–	–
Charge for year	–	40	10
Disposals	–	–	–
31 December 1892	–	40	10
Net book value 31/12/92	650	360	90
Net book value 31/12/91	650	–	–

Note 3: Investments

	Cost	Market Value
Oil shares	£2000	5000

Figure 72 Notes to the accounts

INDEX

A
Accounting policies, 118
  terms, 128–136
Accounts, computerisation of, 51–52
  , drafting of, 114–119
  , layout of, 148
  , preparation of, 99, 141
  , published, 11, 122
Accruals, 107–111, 126–127, 132
Additional costs, 118–119
Advice, need for, 124–125
Advisors, 14–15
Amortisation (see depreciation)
Analysis (see cash book entries)
Appointment, 7
Asset valuation, 129–130
Assets, 12–13, 31, 102–103, 129
Audit, 10, 121–122
  file, 121–122
  trail, 51
Auditor, 14–15, 32, 40, 53, 121, 122
  , timetable for, 122

B
Balance brought down/forward, 47, 100, 139
  carried down/forward, 100, 139
  sheet, 12, 113–114, 115, 116, 134, 153
  , year end, 106
Bank account, 7
    , changing, 55 *et seq.*
      , authorisation for, 56
  mandates, 7–8
  reconciliation, 46–50
  signatories, 7–8
  statements, 10
Bazaars, 94–98
Boxes, 126
Brackets, use of, 126
Breakeven, 86–87
Budget & control cycle, 60
Budgets, 26, 60
Business case, 28, 89–90
    in use, 90–93

C
Capital, 112, 130–131
Cash, 13–14, 19
  book, 7, 10, 11, 33 *et seq.*
    , entries in, 34–38, 40–46, 139, 143, 147, 149
    payments page, 39
    receipts page, 43
    transactions, 105
  flow statement, 115, 116, 155
  forecast, 73–74
  handling procedures, 96–98
  in hand, 7
  , petty, 26–27
  position, 7, 72–74
Charities, 13–14
  Act, 124
  Aid Foundation, 124
  Official Investment Fund, 124
Charity Commission, 123
Check, 114
Cheque books, 7–8

Cheques, 19–20
, signed, 7–8
Commitment, 134
Common investment funds (see charities)
Computerisation (see accounts)
licence fee, 52
Consistency, 128
Contracts, 28–30
Control by delegation, 19
of expense, 25–31
income, 17–25
, principles of, 31–32
Cost, capital, 80–81
, contribution towards, 83–84
, fixed, 84
, full, 83
, marginal, 83, 84
, opportunity, 82–83
, running, 80–81
, variable, 83, 84
Counting takings, 17, 95–96
Covenants, 23
Creditors, 14, 132

D
Debtors, 13, 129
Deposit account, 37, 41, 100–102, 105–106
Depreciation, 112, 131 (see also provision)
Detail (see cash book entries)
Directory of Social Change, 124
Disaster recovery, 51–52
Double entry book keeping, 104, 137 *et seq.*
, theory of, 137–138
Duties, 8–9

E
Expected life, 81–82
Expense claim, 35
, large value, 28–30
, small value, 27–28
vouchers (see vouchers)

F
Financial evaluation, 80–84
position, checking the, 12–14
summary, 77
Floats, 94
Follow up, 79
Forecasts, 86–89, 135
Fraud, 16, 18, 25, 26
Fund-raising, 18
Funds, 14, 119, 133–134, 142
, designated, 133
, general, 133
, restricted, 133–134

G
Going concern, 127–128
Grants, 24–25

H
Hall lettings, 18
Handover, 9–10
Help, sources of, 123–124

I
Immaterial, 135
Income account, 33, 113–114, 114–116, 152
and expenditure, 11–12
Inland Revenue Claims Branch, 124
Insurance claims, 23–24
Investments, 13, 119, 129
, changes in value of, 112–113

J
Job description, 8–9
Journal entries, 105–107, 137 *et seq.*, 142, 145, 150
Jumble sales, 94–98

L
Ledgers, 11, 139, 140
Legal requirements, 119–120

Letter of representation, 122
Liabilities, 31, 102–103, 132–133
Liability, 7, 124

M
Matching, 142
Material, 135
Minute of appointment, 7
Minutes of meetings, 14
Mission statement, 61
Mistakes, 16–17

N
National Council for Voluntary
  Organisations, 123
Necessity, 125
Net book value, 131
  items, 44–46
Notes, keeping of, 79
  to the accounts, 102, 147, 155

O
Opening balances, 104

P
Period to date, 74–75
Permanent file, 8
Petty cash (see cash)
Plan, draft, 62
  process, 59–64
  , running a, 68–69
  , setting a, 70
  , strategic, 61–64
  , working a, 70–71, 76
Planning, 59 *et seq.*
  for disasters, 67–68
  , practical, 64–68
  , treasurer's role in, 68
Pre-payments, 13, 107–111, 129
Presenting figures, 76–78
Price setting, 84–86
Problem summary sheet, 78–79
Provision, 132–133
Prudence, 128
Published accounts (see accounts)

R
Realised, 135
Receipts and payments account,
  99–103, 115
    , deposit account within, 100–102
  vouchers (see vouchers)
Recommended practice, 119–120, 131
Recording decisions, 79
Revaluation, 131–132
Rotation, 32
Ruling off, 50–51

S
Signatories, 7–8, 25–26
Signed cheques, 7–8, 26
Standards, 135
Standing orders, 20
Statement of affairs (see balance
  sheet)
    assets and liabilities, 102–103
    transactions (see income and
      expenditure account)
Status, 15
Subscriptions, 19–23
  process, 21–22
Supporting records (see vouchers)
  vouchers (see vouchers)
Suspense account, 42–44, 102, 107

T
Tax, 124
Tickets, 94
Transfers, deposit, 37, 41
Treasurer as specialist, 72
  , reporting by, 72
  , role of, 87
Treasurer's report, 120
Trial balance, 104, 113, 140–141, 142
    , extended, 142–147, 151
True and fair view, 135–136
Turnover of people, 16

U
Unrealised, 135

V
Voluntary collections, 17
Vouchers, expense, 10
, receipts, 10–11
, supporting, 10, 52–54
, filing, 53–54

W
Writing down, 131
Written down value, 131

RIGHT WAY
PUBLISHING POLICY

HOW WE SELECT TITLES

RIGHT WAY consider carefully every deserving manuscript. Where an author is an authority on his subject but an inexperienced writer, we provide first-class editorial help. The standards we set make sure that every **RIGHT WAY** book is practical, easy to understand, concise, informative and delightful to read. Our specialist artists are skilled at creating simple illustrations which augment the text wherever necessary.

CONSISTENT QUALITY

At every reprint our books are updated where appropriate, giving our authors the opportunity to include new information.

FAST DELIVERY

We sell **RIGHT WAY** books to the best bookshops throughout the world. It may be that your bookseller has run out of stock of a particular title. If so, he can order more from us at any time – we have a fine reputation for "same day" despatch, and we supply any order, however small (even a single copy), to any bookseller who has an account with us. We prefer you to buy from your bookseller, as this reminds him of the strong underlying public demand for **RIGHT WAY** books. Readers who live in remote places, or who are housebound, or whose local bookseller is unco-operative, can order direct from us by post.

FREE

If you would like an up-to-date list of all **RIGHT WAY** titles currently available, send a stamped self-addressed envelope to
ELLIOT RIGHT WAY BOOKS, BRIGHTON RD.,
LOWER KINGSWOOD, TADWORTH, SURREY, KT20 6TD, U.K.